doughBelly's
WISDOM & INSANITY

doughBelly's
WISDOM
& INSANITY

By
doughBelly Price

Taos, New Mexico
1954

Original 1954 edition issued by
Schifani Brothers Printing Co., Inc, Santa Fe, New Mexico

Reprinted by Nighthawk Press, 2023, Taos, New Mexico
with a new introduction by Jim O'Donnell.

ISBN: 979-8-9888976-0-6
Library of Congress Control Number: 2023944452

https://faculty.georgetown.edu/jod/doughbelly/index.html

COVER-doughBelly chats with his old Indian Friend Tony Mirabal.
that was Indian police for New Mexico And Arizonia before the
turn of the century.about the time doughBelly was hatched.

DEDICATION

this little thing is respectfully dedicated to anyone that has the time to read it and the Dollar that it takes to buy it. and the brains to digest what it has to say. and to the good Lord that has allowed me to live through the many years that I spent on the hurricane deck of Bucking horses. riding in rodeos and some on the open ranges as it was when I was A sprout. it is just as I see life these days. what I know I have learned from horses, cattle, Humans and Poloticans. facts, that the great American public hears so seldom now days. it is not copyrighted and any thing that you can do with it to make A dishonest dollar you are welcome. tell your friends if you like it. if you dont Keep quiet. I may want to hook him for A buck.

yours with Malice Aforethought.

doughBelly Price

Taos, New Mexico
December 8, 1954

A New Introduction
to an Old-timer's Book

Was the American cowboy really only invented in 1883 when Buffalo Bill took his "Wild West Show" on the road? It became the stuff of literature in the 1890s, when the German writer Karl May started publishing his books about chief Winnetou (and is still amazingly popular in Germany) and in the 1900s, when Zane Grey became the great American western writer. At least now it's understood that the brightly colored tales of cowboys and Indians and all the imagery that goes with them are at best a vast exaggeration of the brutal life of the American west. But exaggerations, when enough people buy into them, have a powerful truth of their own.

doughBelly Price is said to have gotten his name (properly spelled here) as a chuck wagon cook on the range in the 1920s and 30s, kneading dough on his Santa-like pot belly and leaving behind a coating of flour. He really did spend time on the quieter, settled cattle ranges of his youth, when all the western territories had achieved statehood. Our local sheriff in Maricopa County in the earliest 1900s went off to Washington city as Arizona's first congressman, then shifted to the Senate, where he stayed until 1970: Carl Hayden. doughBelly found his own transition, not to congress but to a real estate office in Taos. That's where I met him, when I was age 9, in 1959 when my parents somehow stopped to talk to him. I was just impressed that I was meeting a real cowboy, as I had been the day before when real Indians showed up on the lawn of our motel to perform ritual dances for the benefit of a folklorist's camera and microphone.

The brutal west didn't last all that long once the lawyers and schoolteachers and farmers and politicians moved in, but the remembered west is still with us and doughBelly was there in Taos to take advantage of it. He sold real estate, but he dressed the part of the cowboy, and in the late 1940s took up writing little columns for the local newspaper, "El Crepusculo" ("Twilight"), and then someone had the idea of gathering them in little books to sell the tourists for a dollar. We came home from Taos with *doughBelly's Crap Book* and picked up his *Wisdom and Insanity* along the way.

In the 1950s, he had somewhat greater ambitions of self-promotion and wrote an autobiography, *Short Stirrups: The Saga of Doughbelly Price*, and the western novelist of the day published *The Diamond Hitch* in 1956, a fictionalized version of the life doughBelly said he had lived. He was, as we used to say, a "character."

We reprint here his *Wisdom and Insanity* to see if we can't give his legend a little life again in Taos and beyond. As you will have seen, he was careful to abjure any and all claims to copyright in his preface, so we don't have to try to track down his estate in order to stay on the right side of the law. We're lucky there, because much of the American twentieth century is going to slip away from us: books presumptively still in copyright with no accessible heirs cannot legally be reproduced, a great shame. When we realized we could let doughBelly speak again, we jumped at the chance.

Please know that he mostly lives up to a certain type of American westerner whom many nowadays think they are emulating when they attack politicians, but doughBelly is a lot milder and saner than the twenty-first century city slickers who try to play the part. He does attack politicians, with a gentle touch, but he's gentle elsewhere as well. He leaves aside questions of racial and class distinctions almost entirely, but his few mentions of "Indians" are all supportive of indigenous people against indignities visited upon them by the white man. He really can't stand Senator Joe McCarthy

– sees clean through him, I'd say. And on the occasions when he does get out of the office to try to sell a little ranch land, you can tell that the white-faced cattle on the northern New Mexico ranges are what turn him immediately to a puddle of nostalgic affection.

So please enjoy this slim volume for what it is, a picture of a picture, so to speak, doughBelly's version of himself and his past and the nation's past, seen from the moment in the early 1950s when terrific change was about to engulf the land in myriad ways. His Taos has resisted supermodernization at least a bit and it's still easy to get out of town – and not all that hard to find a few white-faced cows to spend a little time with. He's a companionable fellow, that doughBelly.

A final confession. I tracked down doughBelly and his works in 1995, at the dawn of the Internet age, and he got his very own webpage long before the rest of us got to aol.com or Facebook or whatever. I gave it to him myself because I was already doing that sort of thing and I thought he'd be fun to show off. In particular, I had found in the University of New Mexico Library, a collection of reel-to-reel audio tapes made around 1950 by a scholar named John Donald Robb. Robb's American story started out in Minnesota and from there he went to Harvard and Yale, then to Paris to study composing with Paul Hindemith and Nadia Boulanger and then lit out for the west. He founded the New Mexico Symphony, was Dean of Fine Arts at the University, and took his reel-to-reel wire recorder, hooked up to his car battery, out to where he could find native New Mexicans who would sing and play for him. His archive at UNM has 3000 field recordings. Late in life, he decided to try something new – I wish I'd met the guy – and took up the MOOG synthesizer, one of the first to compose for that device. I found ten songs of doughBelly in the archive and thanks to the help of Monique Durham of the UNM Library got them transferred to cassettes, brought them back east with me, and got them digitized. When doughBelly's website went up in 1995, it was remarkable for having actual sound files you could listen to. Imagine that, people said, you can listen to music on the Internet! I had a nice time for several years playing the part of the humanist who'd heard of the Internet (the way doughBelly played the part of the chuck wagon cook), going from campus to campus showing off what the web could do. The website's still there, frozen in the graphics and style of that time. If you enjoy meeting doughBelly here, do go and give him a listen: https://faculty.georgetown.edu/jod/doughbelly/index.html

JIM O'DONNELL

JIM O'DONNELL IS A HISTORY PROFESSOR AND UNIVERSITY LIBRARIAN AT ARIZONA STATE UNIVERSITY

A Short Introduction
Emblematic of the Man

In this day and age newspaper columnists exert a powerful influence. Each day we read the innermost secrets of government and politics, straight from the horse's mouth. We read gossip columns filled with claptrap and stale humor; we see Hollywood columns whose contents easily turn the stomach of a hog. We read columns on health and wealth and how to make friends, and joke columns perpetrated by columnists who borrow and never invent

And yet, with all this wealth of reading, how often can we read and laugh, really laugh deep down inside, not only with joy but with the deeper satisfaction of reading between the laughter lines and discovering truth and honesty minus the usual jackass solemnity of the typical know-it-all columnist who preens himself upon his sagacity and thrusts his thoughts bodily upon the reader. How often can we? . . . not very often today.

It is a pleasure, then, to introduce this book. Doughbelly Price needs no introduction to thousands of friends and readers. Doughbelly writes as he lives, in complete honesty, with the laughter that comes from the heart. His thoughts on government and politics are unclouded by know-it-allism and inside information. He writes from the heart and he pulls no punches. You are never in doubt with Doughbelly. You know where he stands today, and he'll still be there tomorrow, and the strange and sometimes wonderful thing is: you find yourself standing with him. On laughter, on honesty, on truth.

This book is filled with laughter and honesty and truth. It will take you back a few years and bring you to the present, and refresh your memory of things past . . . and most important, it will leave you with a clean taste in your mouth and laughter on your lips. No one could ask for more.

FRANK O'ROURKE

doughBelly price Champion bare back rider of California Nineteen twenty five, gentlemenly drunk and dont remember the first three days of the rodeo.

Hello sucker:

Maybe the people that read this little thing will wonder what I do this writing for. the first and foremost is that I think it will bring in more of the E plubris unim than it will cost to have it Published. another thing is that I want the great American public to hear the truth as I see it one more time . . . or the very few that will read it . . . as the truth is so seldom heard this day and time. I had A man the other day to ask me how do you think of all that stuff and when are you going to run out of it? my reply was this: I will not run out as long as they publish the congressional record, and there is poloticians and politics.

most books start by telling who the manufacturer is and when he was hatched. I can cut that short. I was borned in Arkansas, just over the United States boundry line. and I come to be here by the folly of my mother and father and the ignorance of the old time Drs. begetting children is A popular passtime now and has been for as long as we have any history of the human race. and from the increase of the population it is getting more popular all the time.

there is few of my kind (none just like me) left. I sometimes think I am A freak of nature. . . A lone wolf. always squawking about something that is happening here or abroad. but I guess I have got that privelege coming. I have faced the summer sun and winters rain on cow ranches and the same thing on wild west shows and rodeos. Been cold, hungry and had constipation from missing meals and facing A cold, cruel world that neither give or wanted sympathy and no one to write to for money, as My father was A salvation army preacher and was generally in as bad shape as I was when it come to that commodity called money. so it was up to me as small as I was to get something to do that would keep groceries in the Belly and keep the belly from growing to my back bone. I hardly knowed what A mother was.

I have been five foot four inches tall almost as long as I can remember. but I was always like A young cat: all eyes, claws and bristles. and that led me many, many times to over match myself in fistic combats that I had no chance to win. and up till A few years ago I had not realized that size made any difference. the big and bigger looked alike to me. I figured it this way: we was both A womans child, the only difference was that he had got A spring shower of rain that I dident get and just growed A little bigger and that the difference in size was just sap ... easy overcome ... access weight. so at A very early age I faced A cold, cruel, hard world to try and make it over with my two fists. with all the confidence in the world that I could get the job done.

I had very little Schooling. I thought that book stuff was for sissies and mamys boys. and as I look at what our universities and colleges is turning out today I dont know but what I was right. so to start my mission of making the world over I picked the hardest first: the show business with A vacation now and then on A cow ranch breaking bronks. so what I know I have learned from cattle and horses and mother nature, three of the hardest teachers anyone ever had, yet the kindest, most tolerant in most respects. and you dont forget after the first time or two to go up to A bronk from the front, respect the back end, take care of the front end, the back end will take care of itself.

my specialty was bronk riding and bulldogging. I have had people say to me how did you bulldog as little as you are. again I dident think size made too much difference. they might have had the size but I had the guts and that about evened things up as I seen it. I win the championship of the southwest for bronk riding in nineteen twenty five. and the bare back championship of California that same year, and dont remember the first part of the show for I was on A gentlemanly drunk that lasted for several days.

I have seen the inside of many jails. I dont apologize for that, I brag about it. I met some good people in there. the only reason they was where they was, they dident have the Money to hire A good lawyer. guilty or not guilty is errevalent, immaterial and dont pertain to the case.

I think in my very young days my father had hopes of making a sky pilot out of me but he hoped in vain. in my later years, after it was too late, I studied law for my own protection but decided that I was too honest to make A lawyer. I have been charged with most everything and was guilty on most counts. I am just as crooked today as l ever was. Just A little more careful.

my wife had two children. I dont know how many I have got. I paid the pasture bill on one of them and I am very proud of her for she fought her own battles, married well and is doing good. the other one was raised and educated by her aunt, A grand soul, A mother MacCree if there ever was one. never tires of doing something for someone else. and as the evening sun of life dips towards the west we are living the happiest days of our life. we havent got money or I would not be writing this fool thing trying to make some. I dont want A gob of money, all I want is A good living and if I happen to cash in my chips before the wife A little something for her after I am gone, and not too much at that. and should I cash in my chips before I get away from this typewriter I have done more on my own with very little help than most people do if they live to be three times my age. (I am hovering on sixty). when the going got tough and I couldent do what I wanted to do I simply done the next best thing. and at no time in my long crooked career have I went screaming to someone for help. I helped myself. many times to the money and property that belonged to someone else. But I got it by waiting till the sun went down or till he turned his back. tho no one else seems to think so, I think I have done all right.

about the only thing in my life that I am ashamed of is, I run for county representative one time and told the truth. I put on my campaign card . . . dishonest enough to catch the other crooks.

ignorant enough to be frank
noisy enough to be respected
and smart enough not to pass any more silly laws.
I GOT BEAT.

if I had my life to live over I would not change it much, if any. I done the best I could under the circumstances and if I had money I would spend it different than anyone else I guess (I have done everything else different.) I would go from jail to jail and see how many they had in. and I would feed them and I do mean feed them, and then make them A little talk. like this. Now boys you are the forgotten men. if you had friends or money you would not be here. and when you get out I am not going to tell you not to disobey the law. but when you do disobey the law be careful and dont get caught.

the following pages will show you how I think (If You call it thinking). it is just the truth in the raw . . . and some of it is pretty raw. if you like it tell your friends. if you dont like it keep your thinking to yourself. your friend might buy one and you can laugh at him.

TAOS, NEW MEXICO
September 1954

Taking old Bossy to the feed pasture. swearing we would quit in the Spring. But we never quit as long as there was cow outfits that needed cowboys. we old timers all like to look back as we can see farther looking back than we can looking forward

CHAPTER ONE

Try the Attorney

I am in favor of passing A law. (one More wont hurt) making every man that runs for the Senate or Congress after he is elected serve A year in jail. no special privilege, just A number same as the other boys. then he will meet some good people, get acquainted with life. In other words, wake up. that would not be A bad idea to give every man applying for licenses to practice law the same dose. and when he took A criminal case try him and sentence the defendant.

Legal Red Tape

Legal red tape is slowly but surely squeezing the life out of this country. the word legality is sure putting in lots of overtime, and getting union pay for it too. as the American Bar Association is the strongest union in the Country today. BUT we have to have them I reckon. it seems as if they are A necessary evil.

Fourth of July next week, and I bet George Washington would turn over in his grave so fast that you would think he was buried on A revolving door, if he knowed what A mess things was in. all the wonderful talks give on that day will be 5% independence and 95% polotics. Was there ever in the history of the U. S. when there was as many boards? Everyone trying to control something, mostly the taxpayers pocket book. and doing A first class job of the latter.

The only control we need in this U. N. states Is A control on the polotical Parasites. that dont know for sure if the Good Lord was Crucified or shot over Polotics. and the only thing that would kill them is A good hard Honest thought that does not reek of polotics and the party.

Distributors of Confusion

If you caint get into Polotics now you are A dead stinking fish. The D. C. now should mean Distributors of Confusion. Every time they create a tax they create three boards and six jobs at high cost to take up the Tax. and the consumers of the tax payers' money will look at the common taxpayer like A mule at A motherless Colt.

It looks as If this Grand old U.S.A. has got to get along in spite of, and not by the help of the gang in Washington. The time has come for some heavy thinking on the Korean problem. that means Harry will bait the hook and go fishing. Thank the Lord for small favors. If they will let that man Ridgeway alone he will settle that thing. them Koreans Know who to deal with. If it was left to the Washington gang, them Koreans would have to sign A affidavit that they would vote the Democrat ticket next election. That would bring them under income tax. Them boys is too smart for that. Ridgeway will meet them as soldiers, talk common sense--something they will savvy.

Raise – Voting

The only time them Birds in Wash. is ever in the council room at once is when they are looking For A check, or voting themselves A raise. the rest of the time they are out soliciting votes, which is Legitimate cause for being absent on roll call. When they arrive at the Final Destination after death, they will sure be busy for A long time hand shaking with other crooks and pals in come. it will be A hot hand shake.

The roll-back in beef prices looks like the roll was made with Loaded dice, and come Aceduce. well, we have one consolation--It dont affect the old cow any. She will go on doing what comes Naturally, and we will still have beef whether we little insects can buy it or not, it will be here-what we dont send overseas to the Dukes and Dutchesses.

It sure would be A grand Slam if we was to cut off the pensions of them folks, as they would starve in a well stocked grocery and meat market. They are already hollering Sam--come quick in the Iranian oil deal. Sam save the oil or we will have to burn wood—And we dont know how to chop it.

JULY 26TH, 1951 ...

doughBellys Book Goes to the Gov of N. M.

I Autographed one of my gobs of nonsense and sent it to Gov. Mechem. And you know the answer I got showed some signs of Entelligence. He said in part that it had the flavor of you know what, and A vain of humor that was as thick as a corn cob. He is going to recommend it to some of his friends. (I think he means Democrats.) I told him I did not like the idea of keeping gambling closed, as that took some of the butter off my Bread. And from what he said about the boys at Ruidoso I am lucky to have the bread. And of course A line about A vote (as that is all them polloticians think about). If it ever come to A vote on who was the leading Humorist of New Mexico, I would sure have his vote, for which I thank him. But I did not know that Republicans was allowed to vote. He was elected by Democrats.

High Class Club

I am wondering if this house of representatives and congress that we have is not just A high class club that is getting paid by US and Company to muddle up the business of running this Country. the only thing they know in the english Language is Status quo, Jurisprudence, recess and cocktail hour. the Schools they went to taught Latin and Nonsense, and they forgot to learn Latin.

To the Queen's Taste

Some Queen is coming to visit Us this fall. they are making reservations now. that will be on the cuff, charged to the Taxpayers. It will take them from now till fall to get the room cleaned up and all the pictures hung. It will have to be just so--color and all, if it is not right, it might make her Nervous. Never mind the people that has to foot the bill. we have kept the feed bag on some of them Birds for so long now that to take it off would be terrible. And any of us common people could live on what they spend for toilet paper. She will leave this country with unemployment compensation and an old age pension.

AUGUST 2ND, 1951 . . .

Eighty Second Congress Needs Hadacol

Poor old, Tired, Run down, Dissipated eighty-second congress is still Blundering along. Hadacol, where art thou? And what wonders a few tons of Ice water doused into the face of that Gang would do. Every time they come out of the Coma for A few minutes they can think of nothing but raise taxes.

Lobbying Bill

If there was some way to attach the lobbying bill that is paid every year to the National Budget, that would help and maybe cure the ills of that institution. But that seems to be A National sickness that there is no cure for. But the poor things has got to live, and there is A law against Cruelty to dumb animals.

I have said before, and will repeat, it is not what you can Do, But who you can do. Not what you know, but who you know, that will get you places now. they have eased up on the gamblers. So there will be more money for the lobbyist and Contract Getters.

(4)

The Real Estate Cornvention at Santa Fe was A complete success. Ways and means of trimming the suckers better was discussed. Everyone was Painfully sober. And the Cornvention broke up without a fight. Wonderful--civilization is on the advance. The slick haired boys told us common dung hills what to do--get the money honest, but if you can't get it honest, get it. The Main Speaker had served everything But A jail sentence. I had him beat there. And I would lay a bet he is guilty of more than I ever was. The difference is I got the sentence . . . He got the money. Oh, boy, was his hair slick. But that nice Beef dinner they put out tasted as good to me as it did to him.

AUGUST 9TH, 1951 . . .

The Boys Chisel at West Point

Somebody has carried the ball too far at West Point. for many years they looked for both brawn and brains at West Point. But now they have quit looking for brains. If you are six foot tall or better, good looking, and have A way with women, and plenty of pull with some Senator, nothing above the Collar button you are West Point Bound.

You will be taught how to do the chiseling after you get there, and if they cannot teach you how to chisel, you will be flunked.

And it looks like the dribbling went too far in Basketball too. the boys made A long shot and missed the Goal. and why shouldn't the boys take A payoff? everybody else does if the chance comes their way, and if it don't come, they go get it. Just so long as A Man's character is judged by the number of figures in his Bank account, just that long there will be chiseling. They can make laws, appoint the judges, pay sky pilots (preachers) and put Teachers on retirement pension. Have Kefauvers by the gangs, and many of them that is trying to stop chiseling is just looking for A chance to do A little of it themselves. Now what can you expect of the boys?

(5)

Only One Hope

Only one thing to do--that is pass more laws against gambling, then there will be more laws to break. One envestigation to envestigate the one ahead of it, and they all find something new. More dirt A little lower down in the sump. And the annointed few will come out winner. The taxpayer will lose. But there is some hope.

When Margaret's singing gets on paying basis, and Harry gets too old to fish, Taxes might go down a little. I doubt it, but it could be. All you hear now from the consumers of tax money is vacation. But you don't see none of them that produces tax money on one of them things called A vacation.

AUGUST 23RD, 1951 . . .

We Wouldent Have to Try to Buy Friendship If We Cut Off the Groceries

It seems to me like we are buying friendship over in them foreign countries. and That kind of friendship is Just plain no good. If we would just quit sending them the groceries for A while and let them catch their own Rabbits, or not eat and let the slack hide on their bellies Get to where they could wipe their forehead, then when we said something they would not turn up their nose like they smelt something.

As it is, the more we give them the more they want. We have sent them everything, even the president, and they sent him back C.O.D.

Dipos Squirm

Joe Stalin never went to School. that is the reason he is Outdoing all of them Diplomats. if he had A college education he would be Janitor of the Kremlin. as It is Joe is sure making them Dipos Squirm. And industry is getting taxes so high now that no one wants an industry. It looks to me like the taxes is going to defeat their own purpose. Plenty of people will lose A hundred dollars on A roulette wheel, and think nothing about it. But let them have to pay A hundred extra in taxes, and listen to them scream. So the best thing to do is open up the roulette wheels and get the taxes. Look what Monte Carlo is doing. no taxes, and no debts. If that was done in Washington it would not be long till they would have money to Pay the 'Taxpayer.

Look what Wall Street is doing, and look what it costs to get A seat among that bunch of Honorable Thieves. Make Janitors of them Senators and Reps. all they know is Vote appropriations and cocktail hour. They went to School and played Football. no wonder they have no common sense. and that is just what it is going to take to pull this grand old U. S. out of The hole.

Out of the Hole

And I do mean Hole. everything has been Argued in Washington, but common sense. There has not been A case of that reported in that Burg in many years. The more Degrees they have it seems the bigger hoodlums they are. You never heard of an old boy that has to work for a living getting into anything bigger than A drunken Fine. And by the time the Dee Ducts gets through with his check he has got to work another week to buy A small sack of Beans. One can of Beef is all he can afford.

August 30th, 1951 . . .

Standing Law

I see where it is against the law in Washington, D. C., to sell whiskey to anyone standing. I do not know what difference the affect has. Only you cannot tell just how drunk you are till you try to stand. Now it was A very Smart man that had that bright idea. Wonder how many Degrees he has in Science and other things. Encluding the degree that tells you how much you can drink standing and how much sitting on A stool. and how many great Battles was fought (over the cocktail Table) before that one got by the posse of Fundamental rights group. And how many whereases and aforesaids and under yonders was used in that law.

The Radio announced that the envestigation committee was going to take another pot shot at the gamblers in this country. If that was done in dead earnest in the big Capitol there would be A rush for Vesays to some other country by A lot of our top poloticians. And they would want A passport without photos. And mink coats would take A bullish trend.

Senators and Reps Run in Pairs

Them Senators and representatives and lobbyists go in pairs now and spy on one another. One of them will tell the truth some day, and that will close the gambling envestigation, and all the public will ever know about it is A little bitty slice in the paper like this: gambling envestigation closed for lack of funds.

It should read: Envestigation closed on account of too much evidence, and too many involved. no jail space for all of them. And too, this would create A scarcity of Strategic materials. namely: lobbyists, grafters and diplomats. Oh well, I would do the same thing--I guess.

SEPTEMBER 6TH, 1951 . . .

Burying the Indian in the Graveyard in Iowa

Can you imagine anything so small as the Iowa Numbskulls refusing to let the Indian be buried in the city bone orchard? It is A pity that there is so much Ignorance and so many free Schools. That is one time that Harry showed signs of entelligence. If they was to dig up the corpses that is Full blood Caucasian, there would not be A single resident of the bone orchard left. I sometimes wonder if we are not breeding

(8)

right here in the U. S. what we are fighting in Korea. If the brains of them Narrowminded Bible backs was atomic energy, and touched off, it wouldent blow their nose.

Awful!

Well, the crime envestigating committee gave A report Tonight. Awful, Terrible. The crime syndicate reaches all around the Country. Now ain't that A shame! How far does Polotics reach? Pure undefiled Washington, D. C. As pure as the driven snow (now sneeze). But the crime committee dies tonight. we can read its Obitchuary and laugh out loud.

And to be frank, I will lay A bet that Costello come nearer telling the truth than any of them. Some of them birds was afraid someone would tell the truth. And if that ever happens, Oh Boy! there will be wailing and knocking out of teeth. The only way you can tell the Gangsters from the poloticians now is look at their badge. and about the only time they tell the truth is when you ask them what gang they belong to. Nobody denies being A gangster, they brag about it.

SEPTEMBER 20TH, 1951 . . .

My Only Sisters Golden Wedding Anniversary

I missed Squibbs last week (ain't you glad) for the reason that I was in Oklahoma helping Celebrate my only sister's Golden wedding Anniversary. And what A feed--ham, lamb, ram, sheep, mutton and goat! with the gravy just oozing out.

Pies and cake and everything that the brain of good cooks could Conjure up. And kinfolks in droves. And among that bunch of boys of hers (five) I looked like A motherless calf at a roundup. I eat till my little navel stuck out like A pot leg. Baked checken with cornbread dressing. no oysters. just corn bread, some white bread, onions, sage, black pepper. Not this kind that has oysters gommed up in it and all white bread.

(9)

Beef that was cooked more ways than A farmer can whip a mule. There was five boys and four Girls borned to them. and all there. Seventeen grand children and one great grandchild. The girls is no weaklings. Eating started at Noon and lasted till six o' clock. Poor little doughBelly! that is where size cut no figure. I had just as much silo capacity as any of them big boys. And like A bull in a Alfalfa patch, what I could not eat I tromped on.

And believe it or not, No preachers and no Poloticians. Amagine that! One man come in that did not smell right, and went to shaking hands with everybody. I asked one of the boys what he was, and he told me that he was half-polot-ican and half-preacher. But he kept quiet, so I really think the boy told me wrong. that has never happened before.

A Solution

I have A solution for the highway deaths, and fast driving. anyone, And I mean ANYONE And everyone caught driving too fast, or driving drunk, give him five days in the town where caught. pushing one of them Irish Baby Buggies--two handle bars and A fly wheel. (Wheel barrow) around the town with A sign on his back, "I am A speeder," or "I am A drunk driver."

And don't let no man of the legal profession talk his Client out of it. Money don't mean anything to some people. But if they had to do as I have said there would be less murder on the highways and every time they are caught, double the dose. And see that they do it.

SEPTEMBER 27TH, 1951 . . .

Coke-and-Coffee

Them coke-and-coffee jobs is A cinch (if your silo can stand it). Up at eight o'clock. shave, powder your face, paint your lips, have your orange juice. And get to work by nine (if you have nothing else to do). Go for coffee at nine-thirty. Back at eleven. If there is no one that feels like arguing, lunch at eleven thirty. plenty of folks there that has time to argue the next ball game, and how the last pitch should have been delivered. There is just no time to go to the office and do anything before the ball game starts, and it would be sabotage to work while that is going on. very unpatriotic. As soon as it is over they have got to hurry and get ready for cocktails. and dinner. and while that is going on they can watch the Kefauver tribe in action on TV. until they have had so many of them fancy drinks that you cannot see any more and don't care if the war goes on or not. The only thing that worries them boys is how much Harry is going to appropriate the next day. It is sure to be done, but you don't know how much, not that it matters.

Gross Clams Up

The gambler Gross. Did wilfully, maliciously and with Malice aforethought clam up and did not say A thing. And the bribing cops was turned loose in New York. I admire Gross. he didn't desert the ship. and he will not stay in jail long enough to get acquainted with the bedbugs that will be his companions. And if he does he will have the money to get what he wants. There will be many nights that he will not get to bed till the wee hours of the morning. Some of them parties will just have to have him, and his business will require A secretary with him most all the time.

That is not the way my last jail sentence went. and my bootlegging business suffered too. But Gross had money, and doughBelly had time. that just goes to show you what money can do.

P. S. Nobody snores in Washington, as nobody sleeps that sound. each one is afraid of the other, so they sleep with one eye open.

Shaves and Chauffeurs for the Senators

The Senate has approved a bill whereby the Senators can get shaved Free, and the dear Taxpayer is stuck again. Everything is free to everyone except the Man that Produces. But that is all right-them Senators cannot shave themselves after the night before.

And they have Chauffeurs too. paid for out of the Take. I don't know if it is to get them to work or get them home after one of them Cocktail parties that is put on every night, and enserted into the (Taxpayer's) Bill to give fifty thousand more of them Dollars. for expert help to check on Government spending.

Shave the senators, hire them Chauffers, and hire help to check on Government spending. Aint that good? But at that it is the first time Harry has Opened his mouth for less than A billion. he must be sick. A fishing trip would do him good. It will not be long till we hear the cry: "Throw the Rascals out" as we have heard so often before.

Some old joker from Cal. said harm had been done over cocktails and banquet tables. Now when do you suppose that bird woke up? I have knowed that for A long time and I am as Ignorant as A whitefaced steer. But the Demos is holding Harry's hand high as the winner. Some old bird said the Demos stole A primary election in Kansas City. Now that aint all they have stold.

No Sky Pilot

Congress has quit opening with A prayer. no sky-pilots would go there. they should ask some taxpayer to open up the works. He could put up A good plea; not to the Supreme Being, But to them gallivanting Senators and Congressmen.

Durocher In

Harry has put A ban on news. I would too if I was him. his administration background is like my background-won't bear enspection. Oh yes, I voted for him. I am not bragging, I am apologizing. I think we should put Durocher in as Pres. He has A good batting average, and might score A home run. this one we have at the bat is a foul ball in my opinion, which don't change things any. My opinion may not be worth anything but I would sure raise A big squawk if I could not express it. I can remember when democracy was something. now it is just by-laws and constitutional amendments. A horde of money grabbers and fixers Hiding behind the lapel of Justice (I hope). the only time they are happy is when they are going to A funeral or to close the mortgage on some widow-woman's house. Anyway we have got to win the ball game, and the next election.

October 25th, 1951 . . .

Dukes and Princesses Invade the U. S.

Well, the Princess Elizabeth is going to pay us A visit. (God save the princess).

The Duke will take care of himself with the help of the American Dollar, but I am afraid that Harry will not be too liberal in loaning him money. He is not from Missouri. Sure, he will get unemployment Compensation and relief while he is staying in good hotels and visiting Santa Claus. And the eternal Revenue men will no doubt donate him something. as much as they have been stuffing their pockets with.

Some good Old American Farmer that had produced something for them High-hats to eat could go to Canada or any of them places where they stand in line in rain and cold to see the Princess. and they would look at him like A bull at

A bastard calf. Treat him like A step-child and give him A traffic ticket every few minutes. and charge him two prices for A flop. that is the difference between being a producer and A consumer.

November 1st, 1951 . . .

Joe Knocked Out Winnie Knocked In

Two things happened this week that may change things some. Joe Louis got knocked out, and Winston Churchill got knocked in.

Winnie will get to work now on A Pacific Charter. they have one on the atlantic, and another on the Terehan, Yalta. And them other foreign seaports. Why not have one on the Pacific too? The votes was not all counted till Winnie went to work to Borrow money from Santa Claus (U.S.)

Last week was quiet over in them Eastern Countries. they only killed one Premier, or whatever it is they call each other besides names that cannot be printed in the Paper.

And outside of Washington there was one gangster killed over here. They buried him in A five-thousand dollar Coffin. And that may have been borrowed from the R.F.C. That would make A good loan for them boys, stable envestment.

Taft is going to run for president. He cannot be elected. he don't fish and play the piano. two very essential things For a president to do. But Harry will learn him how. For A fee of course.

Tea and Bull

The United Nations rave on. And Joe (Stalin) sets on his single O and grins. that boy has A cinch. And Tho he has no Degrees, he has Brains enough to let The other boys do the fighting. and he gets the profits. Some day Joe will rare up on his dew claws and we won't need help to hold him we will need help to turn him loose. and the U. S. will furnish the men and material. England will furnish the tea. And the Bull. P. S. I am sending the Princess an invitation to come to Taos.

Poor old football-crazy world. Do anything to win the football game. and the radio told how much it cost every year to keep it going. not just in New Mexico, but everywhere.

Water Diet

Well, the union cut off the Milk from New York and made them go on A water diet. whiskey is too high for even the Collectors of Enternal Revenue to drink. Harrys brother, Vivian, seems to have had something to do with F.H.A. In Kansas City, Missouri. He might have his tail in A crack too. But that is all right, he is A brother of the President and raised in Missouri. And had the blessing of the best man Missouri ever had. Boss Pendergast.

One thing about the boss, he paid for what he got, and then got it. No bulling that boy around. If you started bulling him he had men that would gently but firmly lead you down to the creek, give you A nice line of advice, and kiss you and pump you full of bullets. Nice boys. But they got results.

Just look where most of his friends is now. Them that is not shoveling coal down yonder. And Harry can't do A thing about that, even with the help of Winnie. And up to A while back Winnie and Harry could do most everything.

P. S. It's A pitty I was not horned in Missouri. But it had to be Arkansas. close, but close don't count with Harry. If it had Of been Missouri, He would take care of me. and might any way, if I keep spouting off.

Legalize the Games of Chance
so We Have a Chance

I wonder why they don't Legalize Gambling (enternational) . The gamblers had just As well get the money as the R.F.C. and the Revenue Collectors. Encluding the Senators and Representatives. They are all going (tax Free) to South America and the warm countries (No Korea).

Look at this. Redden and Crawford, Congressmen, Dept. of Enterior on domestic Affairs, Has got to go to the Pacific. By way of Paris. Geneva. Cairo. And Bangkock. (A new Kind). The Honorable Crawford Left word that he expected to get back in time to make another trip in Dec. to the Virgin Islands.

Whiskey Hounds

It seems like we have Domestic troubles away from home. Another gang of Algerian Scotch (whisky) hounds has got to enspect the Pacific. To see how much we can loan them. They are five members of the house Appropriations Committee. Appropriations granted without argument. The Eyes have it. And the Congressmen have A nice all-expenses-paid trip. ·they have A hangover from Scotch, the taxpayer has A hangover trying to make A living and meet the Income Tax raise. Good old Faithful work horse (AMERICAN TAXPAYER). And one of the Honorable Congressmen is buying A round of drinks for the house banking committee. to have A long distance look at the bank account of Our dear old Uncle Sam. from South America. That cannot be done in the U. S. That would be too Common. and too, they would have to look (a little) at one of them Common taxpayers that enfest the U. S.

Double Cross

Crosser (maybe old double) Has made arrangements with the Air Force for eighteen (mind you A Dirty dozen and A half) big planes To make A tour of South America. A thirty day trip. From Nov. Tenth to Dec. Tenth. Followed four days later by Another gang of house foreign affairs Committee. Richards of South Carolina is the promoter of that Brawl. He will only take four with him to help drink up all the Scotch in South America. That lusty Gang of Pirates will take the country and never fire A shot. Or lose A man. (Unless it is from D. T.s). At the same time Another gob of Poloticans will leave for Europe. Three Democrats and A lousy old Republican (And the Lamb shall lay down with the Lions).

Crowning Feature

Last but not least, Ladies and Gentlemen, is the crowning feature. the feature of all features. Around the world trip planned by the senate house group. It looks like there may be A slight reason for six of them going. But look what they are Taking along to devour what the six cannot get away with. (they will be like A bull in A china shop. What they cannot eat or drink they will tromp on) As bouncers and Valets: Cox, Reams, Smith and O'Toole. Demo. Judd Ellsworth and Keating Rep. That is odds the Democrats want: four to Three. I will lay my money on O'Toole.

Now here is the final payoff. Another Gang of tax spenders is taking off for two months around (or Drinking) the world tour. Now get this. Five Democrats and five Republicans (the first time I ever heard of the Democrats Giving the Reps. An even break). 'This trip is for the purpose of keeping an eye on federal Expenses. Can you imagine that!

Keep an eye on federal Expenses. I have A different definition and that is to keep the Taxpayer broke. and on the Job. But that goes back to the gamblers slogan. you hear so much--"Never give the sucker an even break."

Stop Polotical Speech Making and We Might Have Peace

Armistice Day thirty-four years ago was called to order. and if Them men would have stopped red tape and speech-making along with the shooting, what A wonderful day that would have been. What this great old United States needs is not more armaments, More airplanes (for war) not more taxes. Not more guns and ships, But what we do Need more of is CONFIDENCE. In our high officials. And that don't take cash.

Federal Fuddling

And another thing we need so bad is less of Federal Fuddling in the affairs of farmers and business men. telling them what to plant and raise. what they can buy for and sell for. We don't live from the Bethlehem steel, and the Stock Exchange. A litter of pigs and A little white-faced calf is what we depend on. And the Federal Government may try to regulate that soon. the young Cows coming on may never have any of the joys of motherhood, except having the calf, when the cow man has to practice Ensemination.

We need more taking care of our own business and less going to the South American countries, trying to tell them what to do. It is A funny thing-we cannot take care of our own affairs, and yet All the Big shots is going to go to some other country and tell them what to do. They maybe can tell them boys what to do, but they sure cannot tell us here at home. THEY DON'T KNOW.

Congress has Adjoined. and Harry is in Florida. Things will straighten out some now. But wait till all the boys gather in Washington and they will throw it in A muddle again. 'This will give the gamblers time to get together A good bank roll. All of the public parasites will be rested, tanned and raring to go. T.V. can have another good play, and stock in Gamblers, Inc., will take a bullish trend. Hear ye! hear ye!

The Good Earth

But the good old cow will still come in to be milked, and the good old Mother Earth will still produce beans. and that is what counts. The rainmakers can practice their fakery. and the poloticians their mystic hokus pokus, but this good old U.S.A. will go along in spite of the Big shots. nothing will keep it on its haunches long. we are too damn Big. every dark cloud has A silvery Lining. If the bright Poloticans will stand aside and let the sunshine through.

NOVEMBER 22ND, 1951 . . .

Poloticans Prayer. Thanks for the Taxpayer

Thanksgiving. and this is the time the boys around Plymouth decided that it was time to get together and count the Indians that had been killed the first year. and how many acres of land had been confiscated when the Indians run out of land. the boys went to getting together as usual. and giving thanks to the Lord for the 'Taxpayer.

I don't find any record of A practical man in Washington. all lawyers and Doctors. if there was someone there that knowed something about practical things, besides red tape and operations, democracy might not be confined to constitutions and by-laws. But become A part of human life.

Beauty Nap

The U. N. laid peace plans before the Russians. Joe grinned out loud and Gromyko laughed all night. that will cost the U. S. for a night's sleep lost and punitive damages. For Gromyko has got to have his beauty nap. Peace plans is going good in Korea. and will till it gets to the political stage and the Dr. and Attys. will mess it all up. One of the gangs will want to wrap it up in wherebys and whereases.

(19)

the other will want to use the anesthetic and operate. One A slow death, the other A sure death. And one Hung Low might not like that.

Is All Reporters Bald-Headed and Pot-Bellied

Spent Thanksgiving in Denver. Visited the Denver Post editorial room. what A joint!

Funny thing, I didn't see A man pounding one of these typewriters but what was either Bald-headed or pot-bellied or both. and almost all of them wear their pants at half mast. like they was in mourning about something. I watched one that had the look of A horned reporter. had that far away look in his eyes like A locoed steer; he had one idea and when it hit him he humped like A cat shot in the rear with A spool of barbed wire. and wrote three or four words, and went back into the trance again.

Caught in the Jam

When you get to the elevator you jab something. and the door opens. I was looking for one of them little cuties that is always on hand, someone said come on. I woke up with A jar and started on in, and here come the door. I almost got caught in the jam. that happened two times. I guess I will stay in Taos where there aint none of them upto-date things. I have almost got my neck in something several times-but not A electric door.

Spent A wonderful evening (it was just after supper to me) with two lawyers and A newspaper man. One of the lawyers was over in Germany at the Nuerenburg hangings. No wonder Goebbels committed Suicide.

Without Gloves

I done most of the talking. and that is the reason I know what the conversation was about. nearly nothing. Bucking horses. some steers and mostly Bull. I handle the Bull without gloves, but it wont stick. it all rolls back on me. Too thin.

December 6th, 1951 . . .

I Go All Out for the Artists

I havent had so much fun since My wife got her ear in the wringer as I had yesterday. Auctioning them pictures for artists. It was A show worth the money, and them little dobs of nonesense sure sold. There was one or two that I savvied. the rest all looked like A chinese puzzle. Some of them of the green valleys and pretty flowers made me want to get down on my all fours and graze like A horse. but as I can see it, the artist should paint the scenes as they actually are--paint it so real that it will make the world stop and think. make it so ghastly and horrible that when the world looks at it there be A longing for peace. dont paint the white-winged dove of peace settling down on this war-torn world, for there cannot be peace until the lust for power and greed for gold is satisfied. and I am afraid that will never be.

the real artist should not try to worship at the shrine of power or prostitute his talent for gold. This goes for writers too. They paint long lines of soldiers marching to the music of fife and drum. the crease in their pants so sharp it would cut your finger. And the scenes of battle. Where some is dying, but in the arms of their comrades. The ensign planting the flag on the ramparts of the fallen foe. The air filled with shouts of victory and things so real that any boy would dream of the world falling victim to his power. of the battle fought, the victories won, the valor wrought, the great deeds done. and all in all it would seem A pleasure not to die in battle, but let us look at the real side of this thing--the side that should be painted. (I understand they would not sell, the public don't want the real facts no more) the destruction of war everywhere. the field is silent--given to the dead. The snow has begun to fall. The eyes that looked out upon the world with high hopes is wide and staring; the body is lying stiff and silent. the dream of the green graveyard at home took care of by loving hands is gone, in its place his bleached bones will be found in the spring, and will not be recognized from the rest. What A difference in the scenes. but A writer writes and A painter paints. do things that will not sell like A modern Lawyer can afford to defend A client that has no money, but both sides of the story should be told and told over and over again till the deafest ear will hear and the dullest mind savvy that not all life is Beautiful and everything that glitters is not gold. this can never be, but we can dream about it.

DECEMBER 13TH, 1951 . . .

Winter in Dear Old Taos

Dear old Taos is so quiet that you can hear the notes fall due at the bank. Highway deaths has slowed up. people has either woke up, hibernated for the winter or run out of money to buy gas. all is peaceful at Santa Fe too, it seems.

But it is Just A lull before the storm. when the first bird, twitters and. sings in the springtime, the poloticos willcome to life with A jar, and things will happen fast and furious. we done this, and they dident do that, but it will be the same little bull that you have heard for years and years. It wont amount to anything. it never has. The only difference is when one is in the other is out. Both sides is looking for one of them Coke and Coffee jobs. and an expense account. When you are in polotics you have almost got to be A crook and grafter. When out, you are an undesirable citizen and liable to be deported, so all you taxpayers can do is just hump up and take it, and hope it dont get too big of A load. But at that it is A great State, this New Mexico-land of sunshine and Pinto beans.

Producers vs Consumers

Well, United States Steel is meeting for a confab on wage raises and as steel goes so goes the nation. And why not. The Steel workers has as much right to a raise as the poloticians has to A pension. and more. They do produce something to make Ships and other things that make this Grand old standard of living that we have and is so much talked about possible. the Poloticians produce misery, and that in great Gobs. The steel workers have got to look out for their own expenses, and have no chance to get anything only what the bookkeeper puts on the check. the polotician has got his expenses paid by the taxpayer, and has many chances to get something that he has not got coming (in lots of cases). I mean the big brass. One of the old stuffy apartments in Washington that don't cost less than Three hundred a month. The steel worker goes home at night he has got to rest. the polotician has to go fight the battle of the cocktail lounge, and admire the Beauty of the Bee girls. But that is hard on the constitution. the Tax muddle is so bad J. edgar Hoover dont want nothing to do with it. now that is getting to be Bad. J. edgar has had jobs that was rotten, but he turned this job down. it must be Smelly, when he cannot stand the odor.

life in winter camp on A big cow outfit. getting in late at night after riding all day
still the supper of sourdough Biscuites and beef to cook. but we liked it.

CHAPTER TWO

JANUARY 3RD, 1952 . . .

We Dont Worry About Steel in Taos – The Houses Is Made of Mud

Taos is higher than A flag on the fourth of July. it has rained, snowed and froze and melted. cloudy and the sun shined. that has all happened in two days--what A privelege to live in that kind of Climate. Met Cabot (silent worker of the Cuspidor paper) and he was grinning like a cat eating liver. Said, this will make grass. I did not know he eat grass. he has nothing in that line. It is so quiet here that you can hear notes fall due at the bank. and that sounds like the peel of distant thunder. Met the Banker (Secrest) coming down the street. Talking to himself. But grinning. second hand car salesmen trading with one another and making good money. I have the best business in the world. nothing to do.

Steel strike dont worry Taos. all the houses here is Built of Mud. go on boys and strike. get what you can. That is what the revenue boys is doing, and the envestigation of them will not amount to anything. it goes too deep. it is gradually dying. most of them is guilty of something, and they look at one another like A mule at A motherless colt. the tax payer being the colt. But there is going to be water in the ditches this spring, and that means grass. and fat cattle. And If I cannot buy beef I can get it. with the experience I have had I will bet I have beef. that is where we have it on the big boys. Most all people here know beef, and all they know is the office. and that is thin knowledge. they might get the money. But that is poor eating. I am in good condition to start fifty-two. I am even with the world. I owe as many as I dont owe. them that I owe can worry, I am not.

Truman Is Either Dumb or Honest – Maybe Some of Both

Every bit of the news we get about the Democrat Candidate for president is that Harry will do the picking. Is he the only one to satisfy in that picking? He wont pick nobody and wont let anyone else do the job. being hard to get is all right. But you can overplay your hand. He will finish up his polotical career in Missouri with A fishing pole trying to catch A cat fish.

But I have changed my mind (light Job) about him. he is either honest or Dumb. Maybe some of both. Poor fellow, he got that job by mistake, and will leave against his will. Just A poor Boy trying to do A mans job. But I pity the man that takes his place. He will have to have the wisdom of Solomon and the patience of Job to get that mess straightened out. and longer than four years.

Womans Press Convention. No Dishes Chunked

Well, it looks like Sunday the 27th will be the final finish of little doughBelly. that day I take charge of the new Mexico Womans Press Association I have not been officially notified yet. I guess they are short of stamps. I did not know anything about it till after it was in the paper. and dont know for sure yet.

But One thing it will be A good finish. Amagine big screaming headlines in the papers, doughBelly killed by A barrage of dishes thrown at him while making A talk before the WOMANS Press Association (with no chance to fight back as it is against the law to fight A woman). IF I survive the battle I should be given the Purple Heart for Heroism. Beyond the call of duty.

I have not made up my mind yet whether it is Bravery or Insanity to take that job. And while I am laying in State the people of 'Taos can walk around me and say (in whispers) he was A good Boy, but he used bad Judgment.

I Land the Cornvention for Taos

Just got home from another one of them Real Estate Cornventions. at Albuquerque. Not a drink takened that I seen. I tried to take the Cornvention by storm, Met strong resistance, backed up, charged again. and landed the cornvention for Taos in Sept. and I am giving warning that if you lose your cash register or anything of value while they are here I swear and declare I am in no way responsible. and if they conduct themselves in A unlady like manner, and blow a safe or two, and don't give me my cut, I will do everything in my power to apprehend the guilty party. and be A witness against them. And I solemnly swear that anything can be proved by me. One recommendation I will give them, is that they are the most lady like gang of thieves that ever put powder in a safe. we split the jack pot for fifty one and made medicine to try to take the Unsuspecting public for all it would stand in fifty two. Selected A trigger man and discussed A mouth piece. But qualifications is hard on that job. He must have polotical Pull, diplomacy. And no Bellium Cerebullium or Mudalla Oblongata. Corns on his rear and none on his hands. any way it was A very Quiet Successful Shindig. Called the secretary of the Chamber of Commerce to inform her of the luck I had landing the Cornvention. and she wanted to hug my neck over the telephone. no dice.

The State poloticans is oiling the big guns to blash Hhhh out of one another. this polotical combat is going to be long and bloody. but all the duels will be fought at long range with toy pistols, so no one will get hurt too bad. it is after the fight that some one will be hurt. No filling for the silo. and if some one dont take care of them, it will be bad, as they dont know how to take care of themselves. when out of polotics.

Jeep Station Wagon vs Cadillac

I am very sorry I made fun of Governor Mechem. about going to Banquets. I am just as bad if not worse. And he can get there so much Quicker in A Cadallic than I can in the jeep. But I can eat more. Goody! I had another round at one of them things Sat. Night. More of the same. Them little Goattie Peas. A dab of them sickly looking Potatoes. like you get fed in jail. A little bit of Roast Beef that was so tough you could not stick A fork in the gravy. But good. as far as it went. This was a get together of the New Mexico press. and I looked like a motherless calf at A round up. the women had on Somer Dresses. Some here, some there and not much where it should have been. Here I am dressed in my Sears and Roebuck outfit. here I go Sunday Morning to make my Grand slam talk to the women of the press. Most of them have been further in School than I have been in jail and that is Way-back. They served milk punch. I just wouldent go for that. I may have looked like A dogie calf, But I drank coffee just the same. it was very pleasant, But I was just a little jittery, but they kept the old temper under control so I did not get throwed out or get hurt in any way. They must have A good feeling toward dumb animals. The talk sounded like A polotician. I promised A lot and delivered nothing. And I left as soon as I got done spouting off so they could talk about me, and there was plenty to say. but look what I am learning. and it is something that you dont learn in Class rooms or lecture halls. and is not given to you with a P.H.D. or a R.F.C. degree. And when I topped the hill where I could look down on Taos It looked like A haven of rest to my weary soul. Even tho Taos is A little Antique I still like it. And till I am hand cuffed and led off, I will still be in Taos.

The Grand Old Man. Abraham Lincoln

Well, the twelfth is the birthday of one of the best men that ever set at the wheel of this Old United States. Abraham Lincoln. He had the wisdom of Solomon, it seems, and the patience of Job. Steered the country through the worst times ever seen. Till now.

And this Korean war job is just dragging along, waiting for the election. And Eisenhower is waiting on Truman. and Truman is waiting for the second coming of the Lord. he is sure it will happen but he dont know the polotical Set up. It seems like everyone in the dear Old Demo party is waiting on Truman.

But there is one that dont seem to give a damn. Joe Stalin. He is going about his business. and doing all right it seems. One radio man will say the USSR is about ready to fold up. the very next one will say that they are building planes faster and better than any we have. That we are running far behind. that sounds about right. We are behind on most everything. but polotics.

Now it is A wrangle over Universal Military Training. What is wrong with that. If it has got to be done, do it now. Something in that way wont hurt that I can see. Sure, all of them countries that has had it went to war. so did we. And some of the boys went too quick. and some of the things that they learn in that way is something they dont get at home. For instance, how to get up in the morning (before noon) some rules and regulations. I dont know but it sure looks like it might be all right. And if something did come up they are partly prepared. Not like the old saying, dont go into the water till you learn how to swim.

Whereases Not Envented

That inspired Book (the Bible) has only seven hundred seventy six thousand nine hundred and ninety six words all told. that is for us to live by, die by and get to the next world by. But congress used over eleven million words in one session. But remember when the Bible was wrote, there was no Ph.D.s and B.A.s. whereases was unknown. and aforesaids was not envented. So the good Lord merely stated his case. No demurrers, and no legal Objections, and he did not have to see the Attorney General. to see if it was Constitutional.

Just take care of your own business. let everyone else do the same. and we could use some of that today to A big advantage. but that would throw A lot of people out of work. Them that takes care of other peoples business as A means of making A living. but we have got them. and If I am so smart, why aint I rich?

FEBRUARY 28TH, 1952 . . .

Legal Profession and Syntax. See Webster

One of the men of the legal Profession in Denver got some of my writing. and read them at A luncheon club dinner for lawyers.. and they said they was most enteresting. he added this comment: Never underestimate the Stupidity of your audience. the best compliment I ever had. in fact the only one I ever had.

had a Woman at the Press cornvention at Albuquerque to tell me that I had to change my syntax. (See Webster. That is what I had to do.) Till I consulted Daniel I thought that was just another Tax that I had not filed A return on.

Being nuts nowadays is not essential. but it sure does help. I lack quite A bit being smart. but I sure am Happy. I have cancelled the future and I am living in the past and as happy as A dead pig in the sunshine.

MARCH 20TH, 1952 . . .

Somebody sent me A clipping from some paper. headlined like this. Danish Mental Institute cures vicious Criminals. Most of them convicted of crimes of violence and Brutality. This institution was started in nineteen thirty five. With three hundred patients. We started one in the United States about the same time. and called it the house of representatives. Only twelve of the original patients is still in the institution in Copenhagen. The rest has been discharged. Of one hundred and forty six that has been finally discharged, only two have returned. This institution here has gained every year. When one is discharged he goes to work pulling polotical strings to get back just as quick as he can. For pickings is good. the only way to lose one is for the "judge of time" to point the long finger of death at him. and that is about the only judge that cannot be bought. where there is no suspended sentence. No demurrers, and no arguments. the only argument is about who will pay the undertaker. The only thing I can see wrong with the Copenhagen set up is the name. This one over here is called the center for Statesmen. In my way of thinking the two places is identical. He goes on to say that once A month the patients is off one day under escort. The balance of the time they are housed and fed. In washington they run loose all the time. And the United States is called one of the enlightened nations. In my way of thinking Congress had better vote A few Million and buy the taxpayers lanterns. and let them spend their time when not working to pay income (at night) trying to find that enlightenment.

We are spending Billions educating our children so they wont have to work. Now what is wrong with work? Is it dishonest? If so, our fathers was sure wrong in what they had to say. and most of them was very dishonest.

Sour Kraut Addicts Take Notice

well, the Queen has arrived (of the Netherlands) long live the Queen. and is that A Break for the Cabbage growers. Everyone in Washington will eat Saur kraut while she is there. so that twangy smell will be in the air. things must be so she will feel and smell like she was at home. the taxpayers had just as well hump up as the touch is coming. them furriners has quit sending he men and gone to sending the women. And Harry was A sucker for the men, and there is no telling what he will give the women. Maybe Fort Knox.

Eisenhower is playing hard to get. But he will be got. and I think elected. And what A job that poor devil is taking on. Taft wont do. he was raised in the·white house. Kefauver is A lawyer too. This Great old U. S. needs fewer lawyers not dumber ones. We have ceased to be A nation of people, and turned into A nation of legality. by a chosen few without the consent of the many. And like the old song, there has got to be some changes made. Eisenhower might be the man, but he had better be A man, for it is no kids job, as that has been tried and dident work.

APRIL 17TH, 1952 . . .

Harry Takes Over the Steel Mills

I have changed my mind just A little bit about Harry Truman. At rare intervals he shows signs of entelligence. He took the big steel company's like the Grasshoppers took Kansas and they are sure Screaming. got the high Priced legal Talent turning hand springs like A turpintined cat to see what can be done about it. they are screaming Socialism, rape, robbery and other things that wont go through the mail in print. Set on your nest Harry. this is one time you are right. got A head of your own. But wherever you want to.

Your statement of the profits of the steel companies shows you are right. After all, this is the day of grab and snatch, so the workers is snatching some too. And why not. The steel company will squall constitutional rights. That has just about developed into what ever the big companies that can hire the best legal talent wants it to be. but the unions is not A baby any more. they have passed the diaper stage. they have some good men too. Thank the Lord. the Farmer and the working man is no longer a yahoo. and demanding and getting some little of what the big companies has had all of for A long time. again, thank the Lord. The cuspidor paper would have to run A sixteen page extra to print what I would like to say to union members: pay your taxes and buy bonds to protect this grand old U.S.A. and pay your union dues (good or bad) to protect yourself in this Grand old conglomoration of big Companies, high polotics. if it was not for unions, you would be working for A ham sandwich A week, and the advice of Fred Harvey would be followed. cut the ham thinner.

Any criticism you might have to offer is your privelege. I say what I want to say without polish or punctuation. and remember this--the hound you hit is the hound that will holler. I am for the under dog. have been one all of my life. The good Lord must have like the under dog, he made so many of them.

when Isenhower is elected there will be lots of them big boys that will be fugitives from justice. they are now, but dont know it. and that was shown when they would not fill out the questionnaire that Mr. Morris was going to send out. If there was not guilty why the objection to filling out the paper. this squibb is not funny, unless the facts is funny. as I see it. Today I am not using my P.H.D. (pile it higher and deeper).

Keep the Dipos at Home and
Balance the Budget

SAY, listen, I am making high Society. I got two letters from the United States Senator (same kind, Same day). Postage free. of course. The Senator dont worry about expenses as long as it dont cost him. (no wonder the U.S. Post Office is in the red.) Twenty years in the senate. that must be A juicy job. or he is A hog for punishment.

I dont see how they have got along in Washington without me as smart as I am. I have solved the tax problem. something that has been worrying all of them for A long time. Stop all these committees. conk them envestigators on the noggin. give the country back to the people. Until we give this United States to the committees and envestigators we had all we needed. now all we have got is first mortgages. the country belongs to the Poloticians and the insurance companys.

If they will give the country back to the people they will build it up again so we can give it back to the Indians. They wont have it like it is now. there is too much on the books against us. If they would make A collection agency out of them senators and Reps. on foreign bills, and turn it in to the U.S. treasury, the Tax Burden would go down like a cob in A cistern. See how much we could collect enstead of how much we can loan.

I dont expect you to believe this, but it happened. I went to one of them Banquets at Sage Brush Inn and got a feed. yes sir. Got A feed. it was really cooked. (something very unusual). you did not have to drink the dishwater or eat the boquet to get full. and then the usual thing--some of them long drawn out gabs. that I reckon has to be. One guy was HEAD of the United States Chamber of Commerce (that little pimple above the collar line dident look to me like it had come to A head). Another one of them Necessary evils. Every time I woke up he was licking his lips or buttoning his coat.

The Montgomery Ward Catalogue Has Not Lost Its Usefulness . . . Yet

The time has come when A man has to wake up every morning with new ideas just like a goose, try to savvy A Eighty billion Dollar budget on top of what we already have on the books. No wonder we are as nutty as A peach orchard Hog. Officials wanting more action--more speed, and more for themselves. we are asked to be A part of too many things. everybody is confused; by the Big words and the loud noise. I think it would be A good idea for us to bring the old outside toilet into focus again. A montgomery catalogue. retire to the quiet sanctuary of that old toilet. the best place in the world to study the more complex problems of life. and today there is many.

Ike is going to be elected. the democrats cant beat him, so Harry is trying to join him and again he is showing signs of entelligence. the crime envestigation--they are going at that backwards (but if one of them high up diplomats was to go to climb A tree he would back up to it) they are envestigating the wrong end. If they would cull out the politicians first and send them where they belong.

Most all of the big time racketerring would stop. Remove the cause and the Disease will cure itself. About the only thing that has not been bribed in Washington is the judge of time. they have not been able to get to him yet, but they are working on him to find out if he is Democrat or Republican and then they will put the Squeeze on him. After this election the sweat on restaurant windows is going to look like beef gravy to A lot of the big boys that has been living off the sweat of other peoples brows for so long. Thank the Lord. I am a democrat (or have been), but right now I am not bragging about it. I am apologizing. But I am just like A woman's mind--subject to change without notice.

MAY 22ND, 1952 . . .

What Is Public Assistance and What Does It Do

I see in the federal budget about three billion laid out for public assistance. what A joke. I dident know the public needed assistance. if they would let the public alone they would not need anything else with jobs on all sides, and more coming up. Why that payout of money. One sure way to kill off A gang of committees in Washington is for several chambers of commerce and other clubs to write and tell them that they dont want no assistance. just let us alone. Them grafters would fall like ten pins. You know I think if we would try to get along on as little as we could, and not try to get all we can to waste, it would not take long for this thing to line up and balance. As for this great bazoo about inflation. Now if this waste goes on A little longer, them same people will not have trouble with the revenue collectors, it will be the welfare dept.

All you hear is universities and colleges. I think we are educating the kids right back into the dark ages. they are educated so high they have not got no sense. oh, I dont want my children to have to work! What is wrong with work? the only thing that is wrong with work today is the simple fact that the working man is the only one that the high tax hurts. the man that pays a million in taxes is not hurt. we all want inflation. it makes things look bigger. like a big shot of dope. we see single and act double. There is lots of people having trouble with the revenue collectors. It is the little man that has got to pay three to five hundred. the big man has plenty left, but they take it away from the little man before he ever gets it. He never gets his lunch grabbers on it (WITHHOLD-ING). This is a highpowered game of confidence that we are playing now. With the confidence all gone. and Uncle Joe (Stalin) and his gang looking right down our throat, with an ace in the hole and another up their sleeve. and our diplomats afraid to get in the pot-afraid that Joe will raise so much that it will not be poker to stay. and still life is one continual round of pleasure.

PPS. My squibbs is getting lots of talk. but no cash.

MAY 29TH, 1952 . . .

Send the Boys Over to Kick the Britches Off Them Foreigners. And Then Send Dipos to Loan Them More Britches

This United States is A great country. we spend Billions. and send men in bunches like Bananas over and kick the britches off them japs and germans. the boys get the job done. and the families of them very same boys has the pay check cut before the man that earned that money ever gets his lunch grabbers on it (withholding) then old Santa Clause takes the dear down trodden people by the hand, loans them money, sends them groceries. And in A way, say boys, we are sorry, what else can we do and how much more can we loan you. We sure want you boys to be satisfied. and this is the second time for germany. (when Germany gets hungry they start A war). I think the chinaman was right when he said, melican he clazy. put hot water on tea to make it hot, ice in tea to make it cold, Lemon in tea to make it sour, sugar in tea to make it sweet. melican he clazy.

In the two good sized combats that we have had in thirty-five years we have borrowed Billions from the taxpayers to spank the boys and more billions to help them get strong enough to give us more trouble. the Marshall Plan, the Dawes and the Young plan cost money, and it also not only cost money over seas, but it give leaks in this country that made plenty of the boys filthy rich here at home. the tax payer here at home had to borrow money on the Morris plan, at several times the rate of enterest of the money loaned out over seas, and is having to pay it back. The other boys is not paying the enterest, and wont. it can never be said of the Americans that we are not sports. The men that loaned money to the boys abroad dont seem to want any of it back. They are the most liberal men with other peoples money I ever saw. It seems to me like we have got the greatest collection of first class con men in the big house ever envented. Soapy Smith and Yellow Kid Weil was pikers. I think the Chinaman was right--Melican he clazy. This is A very exclusive war we are fighting now. The U. N. wants all the credit and Casualties. They wont let Chiang ki Check in on the deal. Oh no, Check, you stay out, your boys might get hurt. I just dont savvy.

June 5th, 1952 . . .

The Most Unpopular Nation
– Korean War Prisoners

Our great leaders have bought the united States A grand stand seat behind the eight ball in the great crisis of the world today. They have tried to buy friendship and confidence, and that is the one commodity that is not for sale. We are the most unpopular nation in the world. In Korea there is thousand behind barb wire that is telling the U. S. Army what to do. I don't know who is prisoners of war; the reds or the U. S. Army. There can be no peace till there is satisfaction; and the world is not satisfied. and getting worse all the time. We dont need diplomats and B.S. degrees, we need some common sense. the great American Public is living on the installment plan and the payments is harder and harder to meet, as the foreign countries is setting the terms on that installment plan. and paying less taxes than we are.

we have to win wars, build our allies up and put the people
we spanked back on their feet, and they are now telling us
what to do and how to do it. They have our diplomats by the
seat of the britches and A down hill pull got them turning
around so fast they can see the back of their own necks. and
getting exactly nowhere. The foreign countries is hungry for
groceries, we have that. This United States is hungry for
leadership, and it looks like the old womans biscuits at the
hotel . . . there haint any more. In the newspaper there is
one short column about the war in Korea; five columns about
the presidential candidates. And three about baseball. two
about scarcity of things here at home, to make the people go
further in hock for something they dont need. and the pay
check now wont reach from one pay day to another. Scarcity
of steel that is a joke. there is millions of junked automobiles
that has the very best steel in them but I reckon we will have
to ship that to Russia when she says for us to. Joe may be
Illiterate, but he has got plenty of what it takes to tell them
boys with the long degrees what to do, and they are doing it
too.

JUNE 12TH, 1952

The Shot Gun Wedding of Germany and France

I am just one of the millions that dont savvy this de-
fense talk. In the last Combat it was too little and too late.
Now it is too much and too quick. from the way the dipos is
whooping it up, it looks like Russia is stronger than Japan
and Germany both. The production now is as good as it was
at the peak of the last Combat. it looks like the Russians
Might is like my bank account--overdrawn. I think the men
in washington has the spending DTs. I never had that kind,
but I have had the other kind. and it makes you see things
and do things that will not or cannot happen. the rearming
and Tying Germany to France has all the ear marks of A
shot gun wedding. trying to make the lion and the lamb

(39)

sleep together.

It might work--stranger things has happened, I guess). That isenhower is batting A home run every time he picks up the stick. go on, boy, you allowed it to be lawed off on you. I think you will get it; I think you will want help to turn it loose. You could tell one of them G.I.s what to do and he would do it. But when you tell one of them Poloticians what to do he is liable to do anything or nothing. and if he does do something it will be backwards.

It dont look like Ike is going to split the Texas Delegation with the Taft Boy. thats A boy, Ike, go winner takes all. and I would not be too careful about the Marquis of Queensberry rules in this fight. and not be too particular about breaking clean in the clinches, as this is A finish fight, and it looks like it might be the last one for the Grand old G.O.P. if they dont win this one. and it aint going to be easy.

But stay in there and fight boy, Ike. I have had several letters about the squibbs. It seems like people like to read it. and dont savvy. and what they do savvy they cannot digest. And it might be just A little complicating above as well as below the belt line.

JUNE 19TH, 1952 . . .

The Cow Business on Rubber

Well sir, the cow business has gone on rubber wheels. the cowmen has sold the cows to buy trucks and cars, the milk he drinks comes from A pasteboard bottle and the cream for coffee from A pet cream can. it is too much work to milk A cow that is done by machinery, and work never hurt as many people as Schools and colleges where the grand idea is pumped into their hollow heads that work is for that that dont have A degree.

There was A time when you never heard of that juvenile De something. the kids had something to do . . . get in the fire wood, Cut kindling, feed the stock, enstead of coming home from one of them Institutions of insanity. And do the houdini disappearing act on a Gorn of groceries. and thumb their nose at the mother. and go to the baseball ground or to some moving picture show to see hop. Cassidy bang out the two gun act. and kiss the STAR till it sounds like A cow pulling her foot out of A bog. or hear Johnny Ray (Cry) sing, and that sounds like A lonesome coyote on A high hill, or one of them wailing Soperano Screams. If that is music I am a chinese aviator, and out of A job.

My honest opinion is that the American Public is A gang of over-educated half wits In book learning, and as for the practical side of life, dont know if the Good Lord was crucified or pushed from A aeroplane. and too smart to learn. and the way them so called illiterate Russians is putting it over us is what makes me think so. Joe Stalin is setting back with that illiterate grin on his face like a cat eating liver.

I guess I was borned too quick or too late. That old mammy that cut the gee string that severed me from my mother (the Dr. was two days late) should have bungled the job. Maybe she was crosseyed and spanked on the wrong end.

The boys has won every war we have had in the field, and the diplomats has lost every one at the Conference table, so it can be seen that the ones that win the wars is the old slogging foot boys. and that is where degrees dont count. who lost the wars? the diplomats that has the long, high sounding handles hung to their names. With their Bungling we have finished behind the eight ball every time at the Palaver table.

June 22nd, 1952 . . .

Little doughBelly Refuses the Smore Grass Feed — Wants to Dunk His Hard Rolls in Coffee

Sunday, June twenty second, just got home from the State Press cornvention at Santa Fe. And say, did I mix with the congregation of the wise. At the cocktail hour (uninvited) I met Hal Boyle, columnist for four hundred papers (three hundred and ninety nine more than I write for). He is just womans child like I am, only bigger. I did not notice any over supply of knowledge oozing out of his ears.

I looked like a dogie calf at a round up, and I guess felt about the same way, among that bunch of old bulls, with my broad shoulders and big hands, Clark Gable profile and little protruding belly. I kept quiet, something unusual. But I know when I am outclassed. It was a grand collection of sham and shallow pretense, as I seen it. But maybe I dont know.

I did not eat with them, as I shore like to dunk them hard rolls they hand you at them places, in my coffee, and that is not poker at all. And too, I never eat one of them smore grass boards feeds. So I just splurged and went and eat a beef steak, I know what that is, and I got fried potatoes, I know what they are too. But them hog rotten kind I am not sure.

It was a grand collection of rounders, roughnecks and hack drivers. All dressed in their sunday best, that didnt fool me much. But I enjoyed every minute of it, and left on my own power, in other words, didnt get throwed out.

JULY 3RD, 1952 . . .

G O P S Is Kicking Ike's Pants; They Dont Want a Man They Want a Polotican

It shore looks like the dear old G.O.P.s is forming a rugby huddle to give Eisenhower the bums rush at Chicago. Neither party wants a man as president. They want a polotican. They dont want brains--they want diplomacy. Diplomacy has never paid off. Brains has never been tried. A Diplomat is a bronk rider with his brains kicked out. It has been so long since we had a brainy man in the lead that definitions has been forgot. If it could be defined it would not be understood, and if understood it could not be digested.

We think we are the captain of the greatest ship of the world. And we are just cleaning the deck for nations that we have paddled. When we got Germany whipped, our smart boys gave Uncle Joe Stalin the winnings, and he has been playing with our money ever since. We think we are leaders, we are buck privates in the rear ranks. The two head McGimpers that went to Yalta and Pots dam, damned shore had the give away blues. They give Joe Everything he wanted and seemed put out because he didnt want more. They set the stage for Uncle to act on and be the number one thorn in the peace plans of the world. When you set in a game with Joe you had better play them close to your belly, the two presidents set in the game with him, with plenty, and come out with only the pocket the money was in, and was lucky to have that pocket. And yet Joe dont know nothing. He was kicked out of kindergarten for not shaving. You know that good old hard common sense and brains would be good now for the whole United States if takened in large doses, both internal and external. When our leaders in Washington make a mistake, instead of admitting it, they deny everything and make three more mistakes trying to cover up the first one.

JULY 10TH, 1952 . . .

Pan American Air Ways Go On Relief

Times is sure getting bad. Pan American Airways has gone on relief . . . seventeen million worth, and some of the Churn heads we call Senators and Reps. fought the Appropriation till a champagne Party was give by the Officials of the Pan Am Co. It was there that the Officials of the Pan Am and the dissenting Sens. and Reps. kissed and made up (for A fee) and lo and behold the seventeen million bucks was donated. no one seems to know what for, unless it was to show the taxpayer how to save money.

The precornvention fight In Chicago is looming up like

a red vest on a fat man. they are kicking Isenhower in the seat of the pants so fast he thinks they are patting for him to dance. that is diplomacy. He is the only big man that has ever went to Europe and dident bring back a new mortgage on the future of this country. Taft has a grin on his face like the wave on A slop bucket. The democrats (if give A chance) could elect a good man for president this time (Isenhower).

P. S. If Taft is nominated 'Truman will be the next President, as it will be easier to beat Taft than it is to move Harry's piano and dont get your bowels upset, he wants it. the draft wont have to be very strong.

JULY 17TH, 1952 . . .

G.O.P. Shows Signs of Entelligence.
Ike Is Nominated

The dear old G. O. P. showed signs of entelligence. They have got A man in the lead that is A gentleman and A Scholar. One thing he aint (yet) is a polotican. He is starting without handcuffs on. He can wipe his nose with one hand and point the finger of scorn at the democrats at the same time. One of the Filthy rich Demos popped off and said the Republican cornvention was the greatest show of confusion, corruption and Conniving he had ever seen. He has not been A democrat long, I guess. the demos is not simon pure. They will start their carnival with A prayer (some taxpayer should give the prayer, he would know what to ask for) and close with A fistic combat. when Isenhower was kicking the britches off of Taft, Truman said he was worried. I wonder why. no one can do any worse than he did. He has give A first mortgage on this United States that will last for many years longer than I will. the best that the next man can do is give A second mortgage, and the banker told me when I tried to give A second on my home to pay income tax With that A

(44)

second was no good.

the thing to do is elect Ike. let him take care of the parasites over seas. put the leaches in washington on the relief rolls (dont let them starve, it would be cruelty to dumb animals). Give American back to the people. stop this living on the installment plan. dont let A automobile on the highway till it is paid for. In short, pay when you get it. Give them boys over seas all the groceries when paid for. It wuld not be long till the Government would be having to pay the taxpayer. When the smart whitemen took this country from the indians there was no debt--no tax--the women done the work, but he was so smart that he went to giving out scholarship degrees, and look what A mess it is in now. And the indians was called Illiterate and Savage, and they call this the age of enlightment. Funny, aint it?

There has got to be some changes made. Some common sense in Washington, and less degrees. Somebody that will take care of America enstead of the party. See how it works to put more into the Government than is took out. Not make Uncle Sam do all the blood giving. Give him A transfusion once. As it is, the great ship of Zion (U.S.) is headed for A stormy voyage and A rough landing.

P. S. I am so Smart I dont see why I aint rich.

JULY 24TH, 1952 . . .

Democrats Take Chicago. Dont Fire a Shot or Lose a Man

The Democrats is taking Chicago like Grant Took Richmond. Rounders, roughnecks, hack drivers and five percenters. dont let that upset you, they are not going there for the good of the country. It is to try to keep A strangle hold on that job and still suck that old polotical teat that has kept them from dying the slow withering death of A water moccasin, and the great Conquering Hero Harry S. Truman in the lead. The Napoleon of the Missouri cornfield. he grabbed for the engine and I think might get the Caboose (maybe) this time. His polotical star that rose so bright under the Direction of boss pendergast will sink this year under the onslaught of Ike Isenhower. I have a slogan for the dear old Democrats this year: IKE IRKS ME. I should get paid for it but I bet I dont. the great Invincible machine that he and others has built has begun to creak at the joints, the drivebelt is out of line, the carbureter is flooded, and the transmission is dry.

They will not break no speed limit this time, the democrats is big giants, but they are on thin ice and fighting amongst themselves. if they break down and go to telling the truth on one another. Oh Boy!

Taxes as of now is a fifty fifty split between Government and the business man--the Government gets the taxes, and the Business man gets the split. The Gov. gets the money, the Business man gets the enventory that has still got to be sold. If he cannot sell the enventory for profit enough to live on he can go on welfare (lingering starvation). Today if you want security from want and income taxes, clothes to wear, worry over Dr. bills and safety from these low flying enstallment-bought Automobiles, join the Army and live happy ever after. if you want to lay awake nights and worry, get you A business. Get Married. Get Hungry. And have A string of tax collectors following you all the days of your life, and dwell in the house of Discontentement forever, but with all the poloticans and crying I do, I still like this old U.S.A. Especially New Mexico. and as long as the white faced calves keep bawling, and the little pigs squealing, we are all right. Let the delegates wrangle. That is all they know, and may they nominate the best man. It dont make no difference, he will not be elected anyway.

Degrees and Levi Garrett Snuff

Hump up, voters, here is the verdict from the democratic side. they nominated A bird that has more degrees than Levi Garrett has snuff. he even went to switzerland to learn how to get A big retainer fee. Harvard and princeton finished the job. Great gobs of wolf bait, caint they get A man that has some sense and not so many of them sheepskins. And they had to draft him (Oh yeah). I had the honor of being drafted one time by A federal Judge. to do ninety days in jail.

The demos is getting hard up when they have to make A man take the job. Harry wanted the job but he knowed he couldnt win. He can go back to selling neckties and fishing. and playing the piano. The R.F.C. will finance him shorely. Ike is in Colo learning how to catch Suckers. and I think will catch enough Democratic suckers By election to win easy. He may not be any better than what we have had. but he will be different.

The New deals, fair deals and second deals has sure been worked over time lately. If the cost of this campaign was put on the budget it would balance this year. It is costing A thousand dollars A minute for them birds to spout off and be seen on Radio and TV and that is A wee Drap in the kettle. Special trains whistle stops and other gifts. If I had the Scotch whiskey bill I would not speak to either one of the Candidates.

Stevenson said he did not want to be Pres. at that very time he was having close communion with the great polotical Boss Arvey. and it is A safe bet that he had the Sanctimonus nod from the Napolean of the cotton patch (Harry S) to get going. and that was long before the cornvention. neither one of the Candidates can claim kin with washington when it comes to telling the truth.

Amagine A man not wanting that job. That he and four other generations has lived from vitimans of polotics. If you are making arrangements to have heaven as your home when you die, you will not have to associate with either one of the presidential Candidates. Ike was going to cut taxes fifteen per cent. But he has an out. He dident say when.

Arabian Prince Abdullah El Faisal Al Saud (how many horses did he have to steal to get that name) is in Santa Fe. three weeks health tour. Now that is just A educated way of saying they are here to fill the old silo with good american groceries. And tap Sam for a Loan. He looks like he needed to float A loan from R.F.C. for the price of A shave.

August 7th, 1952 . . .

John L. Lewis Puts the High Brass to Wiggling Their Ears

It shore looks like old Bushy Brow (John L. Lewis) is going to hump and take another grab at the coal users pocket. This wave of prosperity is going to put us all on welfare. As for me, I had just as soon see it go to the coal miners and steel workers as the poloticans and revenue boys.

I would make the suggestion that we close all the coal mines and gas wells and go back to using cow chips, but the cattle now is so high bred and got so many things shot into them (vitimans and Vaccines) that the chips wouldent burn. It takes grass and vegetation to make good burning cow chips.

I know these strikes and enternal combustions in the U. S. is doing one thing-it makes Joe (Stalin) happy. The pill-shooters (Drs) say a good laugh is fine for digestion. If that is right, Joe is sure not constipated. And we are giving him the laughs. I have a sneaking idea that getting Isenhower nominated did not suit so well, but all he has got to do is voice his disapproval. That is the only thing that will beat Ike.

(48)

I had something in the clip joint the other day and I dont know just what it was. He was either a duke or a devil, maybe both. I went to spreading him my line of bull and he looked at me like a mule at a motherless colt. He told me something in several different lingoes, some English among it. Very badly chopped up, and walked out. I was glad to see him go.

I speak several Lingoes myself, some English, plenty of profanity, through my nose and slang. But I did not get his line at all. Just as well, I guess, he might have wanted to borry something. He could have been an artist or a writer, or some other uncommon nut. He was holding on to a very entelligent looking dog. Just another species of the Good Lords Neglect. No doubt he thought the same about me.

That is one thing about this country. You can think what you want to and dont have to ask the County chairman.

AUGUST 21ST, 1952 . . .

A Rodeo Without Fights. No Drunks, No Spurs. And a Strained Feeling.

Went to the Las Vegas rodeo last Sunday. and be it resolved that antonio Lopez De Francisco doughBelly Price is not going to form any big habit of going to them shows.

It was A good show from the grand stand point of view. But nothing like the shows I went to in the days gone by. I never seen A fight--Never seen A drunk. When I went to shows we went to try to make expenses. and have A good time. You always seen one or two fights each night. and had one or two that you dident see. Got beat up, bucked off, tromped up and had A wonderful time. but at this show ever one seemed to be so Busy trying to make the income tax that he dident have time to holler.

I win that show In twenty five and should have felt at home. but there was A strained feeling. Not only me, but

(49)

other old timers as well. I met some of them. Old Dee Bibbs, the Laughing Hiena. and the old steer roper ike Rude. He talks so fast and so loud, Edisons Phonograph would be A dummy when he was there. he is still going strong. and say, when he spreads A loop there is liable to be beef on the other end of the rope.

But the old time cowboy is fast answering the last call and they aint making no more. like the cattle of today, they are getting streamlined. In the old days they put the brand on A calf, now it goes on paper. they have bred the horns off of cattle and spurs off cowboys. and when you want to turn the bulls in with the cows you have to have An order from the United States dept. of Agriculture.

We used to change horses three or four times A day on roundup. now we change oil in the car. pull the steering wheel enstead of the saddle horn. adjust the seat instead of the stirrups. the picture has changed. But I have not. Borned too quick or too late. But the fact that I am here is proof that I was borned. GOODY.

August 28th, 1952 . . .

The Great Battle of the Cocktail Lounge
No Casualties. A Good Hang Over

Well, the poloticus boys is oiling the big guns and polishing the side arms. getting set for the great battle of the cocktail lounge. There will be plenty of blood shed in that battle. but it wont be red. dont worry, it will be the same old story (S.O.S.) only have A little different smell (it never did smell like cologne) .

Ike come to New Mex. Not polotical. But it had A strange stench of something rotten. If Ike wins this election, the Missourians fleeing Washington and the polotical jobs they have had so long will look like the retreat of the grand army of Napoleon from russia. welfare rolls will take A bullish trend and corn bread will again get A good play.

The Justice Dept. envestigation died A terrible death. like I said, it would, weeks ago. For this reason, who will envestigate the envestigator. that is the question that stopped the Legal profession, and they are hard to stop. there was no precedent. and where that thing is lacking, there is no nolle contendre. Corups delecti purse or Status quo in Toto. Oh Boy, do I spit the lingo. But I have got to have A lot of respect for them. for I have went to court when I just could not have justice. and they are the boys that can keep justice from throwing you so far in jail that they have to shoot beans to you with A choke bored shot gun.

In regard to the enternal Revenue Dept. and them boys. I suggest that there be no books kept. then no one would know how much they take. and there would be no worries over it. they are going to take it anyway. But you cannot blame the poor things, as they have got to keep the higher ups living (up to standard).

It seems to me that the standard of living curls around just A little. the man that eats T bone steaks dont know if A cow sleeps on the ground or in A tree. and the man that raises the T bones eats what he can get. and after Income is paid he is lucky to eat at all.

P.S. Adali S. Truman is sure whetting the knife for Ike. But there will be no blood shed.

SEPTEMBER 11TH, 1952 . . .

doughBelly Was the Ghost Instead of the Host at the Real Estate Cornvention

Well, the State real Estate Cornvention has Passed. With as nice A gang of heisters as ever put powder in A safe. I was Host and I think there should have been a "G" in front of the host, as I was not there too much of the time. But I did hear some of the talkers. A professor or something from

(51)

the university of N. M. he dident say too much. and what he
did say dident amount to much. my opinion is when he was
getting his degree he should have been getting A sentence.

Another man--I dont know what he was--sounded at
times like A man of the legal profession. After hearing them
men I have come to the conclusion that there was two things
that I could have been if I had of been different. One was A
lawyer. I was too honest for that. and the other was a Prof. I
was too smart for that.

Seasons of the Year. Football Baseball Basketball and Vacation.

I still insist that this country will never come out of the
red until common sense is used enstead of diplomacy. This
great country was founded on common sense and got along
fine till Diplomacy took over and now we are in one helluva
shape.

Whoever is elected President had better try to take care
of the United States and let the polotical party take care of
itself for a change. And bring satisfaction back to the country. For when there is no satisfaction there cannot be peace.
Get our schools back to teaching such simple little things as
what the four seasons of the year is. Spring, summer, fall
and Winter. Now the four seasons taught is Football, Baseball, Basket Ball and vacation.

Teach them not to judge a man by his bank account or
the high falutin language he uses, but what he has above the
collar line. And that is not learned in class rooms and lecture
halls. I believe in giving our kids A chance. but not A cinch.

Give America back to the people. Give the man that has·
money A reason to expand. That will make jobs bring satisfaction and peace will come automatically. In other words,
remove the cause and the disease will cure itself. As it is
now, the man that has money dont know what to do with it.
and the man that aint got any, caint get it.

Ike Has All the Honesty There Is Left and Will Lose That When He Makes the White House

The way beef on the hoof is going down and beef over the block is going up it won't be long till we had better not offer the cowman even A five spot for it sure will be took. The loin of A beef cut in thin slices will cost more than A whole cow on foot.

And this registered stuff . . . I don't savvy. A good grade, white face, nine hundred pound steer will make just as many thin slices of beef as one that all of the ancestors has been registered. Them Registration papers is poor eating.

Beef is just good for one thing (manure) human consumption. and when it gets so high that the man that raises it can't eat it, the boys that can buy it will get gorged out. Yes, we have parity but that is not very good to eat unless you have plenty of cream and Sugar to go on it.

Adlai S. Truman said that no party had A monopoly on Corruption. That is just right, and I will add that there seems to be no monopoly on Honesty either, for their ain't enough left to bother with. Ike has what little there is left, and he will lose that when he makes the white house.

These freaks of nature called poloticans is funny things as I see them--specie of the lords neglect. Taft got beat but just like A Oak leaf after frost--Dead, but still hanging on. Like A pouting school girl. If you don't let me chew your gum till recess, I wont show you my sore toe. Why don't he get A route card and get with it. He ain't satisfied with throwing the bull, he wants to be the bull.

If he had of win the nomination he could not have run fast enough to get hot. The voters of today is tired of politics--they want brains. Some one that can organize the people, not polotics. Everybody is confused. Like the blind men at the nudist gathering just feeling their way around.

Harry is starting his whistle stop session soon and his final stop will be Kansas City. selling neck ties. The american people don't need a leader as bad as they need to be let alone. Debts is not hurting this country as bad as the traveling expenses of the diplomats.

Ike Can win if his henchmen will let him alone. As it is, there is A lot of them riding his coattail and dragging their feet. But the election won't hurt so bad if congress dont regulate the cows having calves and the sows having pigs, the big boys will eat T-bones and the little ones Chili. But chili is good. It may be hot the day after, but good just the same.

The dear old Demos is sure screaming -- Ike is stealing our platform. They should holler about some one stealing something-the platform is all there is left to steal and it needs new planks, so Ike is getting very little when he steals it.

OCTOBER 9TH, 1952 . . .

Who Chiseled Sam. Everybody.

This was A promising campaign to start with. Promises of reduced taxes, more old age pension, in fact security from the enjection to the resurrection. Then you are on your own. Then, and not still then, will thecandidate desert you. But it has turned into A financial statement. And who has chiseled on whiskers. It don't seem like it matters who has, but how much (they all have) chiseling was done.

Everybody does, and why not the top candidates. They are human too. Both top men talk about honesty in their party. Honesty in either party is nothing but A disease and no one in that game has ever had it. But top men seem to be holding back something. The democrats is scared and the republicans is glad of it. Except Harry S.--he is stomping around like A bull in A china closet. His whistle stop campaign is not going so hot. The American public has heard the wind blow before. He says that Ike is A front man. We need

A front man. We have not had one for 20 years.

He also says Ike is not A polotican. Thank the Lord for small favors. We have had them things for twenty years and look where we are at--Behind the eight Ball. If Ike wins this time, second story windows in Washington will rent high. For the defeated democrats to jump out of. The undertakers should all vote for Ike. The dear Demos has stopped the rich gravy so long I doubt if some of them can take it. Ike will stop A lot of them from chiseling on income. Just stop the income. And go to the university of alcatraz for replacements.

He might have trouble finding A republican there but if he did find one he would be A good one. I sure hope the boys get their financial statements ready by the fourth of Nov. or the election will have to be postponed. Accountants take notice.

OCTOBER 16TH, 1952 . . .

Back on Home Ground. Pleasant but Old Memories

The first of this week I was over on the A Six ranch where I broke bronks and punched cattle in nineteen twenty-two. A cows' paradise-plenty of water and grass, and I looked at fifteen hundred head of the Fattest white-faced steers I have seen in A long time. And the most contented specie of the lords creation I have seen. It was so different from looking at A gang of we smart Humans. Them steers was not worried about the world serious baseball game. The presidential election or the war in korea. They was not registered, they was fat. Had never been Combed or rubbed down. And lived on the open range where A steer is supposed to. And could look you straight in the eye--something that most humans cannot do. They had done nothing wrong and cheated nobody out of anything. They have got sense. They eat, drink and lay down.

We smart specie of the Lords neglect eat and drink and

then go to looking for somebody to beat out of something. or go to some Bar and take on plenty of the algerian sheep dip. Get in the car going home--get on the wrong side of the road--shut both eyes and drive like hell and hope we get there and we are called smart.

In another pasture was the mother cows and calves. Them little white faced calves running and kicking up their heels was A sight to behold. That was mother nature in all her glory. No sham and shallow pretense there. Nature in the raw as it should be. Them cows was teaching the little fellows how to take care of themselves. And letting mother nature take its course. The wise, kindest, most tolerant teacher that ever was. None of them cows have degrees. They have brains. There was consolation and contentment in looking at them cattle. But what A difference when you look at that many so called entelligent Humans. And the hurry, strife and false smiles that they give you while they try to get their hand in your pocket. But such is life!

OCTOBER 30TH, 1952 . . .

Order a Dollars Worth of Steak Now All You Get Is a Smell of the Butcher Block

Beef on the hoof going down, and over the block going up. In A butcher shop now all you get for A dollar is A smell of the block. Where is the slack going? And old Bushy Brow (John L. Lewis) has humped up again. That boy has sure got the poloticans on the run. When he says rabbit they wiggle their ears. and start hopping.

In polotics you must be A crook and A grafter. Out of polotics you are an undesirable citizen and subject to deportation, as honesty in that game is A miracle. One of the big shots (Sparkman I think) has had one of them nervous tear downs. The pill shooters called it Larangitis (whatever that is), but he can't talk, poor devil. It is A shame that that

Disease is not catching. But most of that Bazzoo will subside like A bromo seltzer in A few days. Half of them will be in the class of the also run, and be like the little boy the bull butted--have no say coming. Then we can get The news of the korean war and how many has been killed on the football skirmish line. This is sure A funny world, but I sure like it. We are all suffering on account of too much comfort and don't know it.

NOVEMBER 13TH, 1952 . . .

Democrats All Gone. There Haint No More

Eisenhower took Washington and never fired A shot. And I have not seen A democrat since Wednesday morning. Harry Truman was the best Campaigner that Ike had. People dident vote against Stevenson; They voted against Truman. Adlai was blowed up higher than A flag on the 4th of July. But he shore come down with A deep thud. Harry said Ike dident know anything about polotics. Shows Harry was not so smart himself.

The reps slapped the demos down like A wet sock. They are going to reorganize the Vigilantes in Missouri to take care of the displaced Missourians fleeing from Washington. Harry says Ike can't do any good going to Korea. How does he know? He never tried it--he went fishing and played another tune on the piano. The people wanted something new, and could get A free vote, so they just dabbed down and bought the republican party for four years. Votes is the only thing you can get now that there is not A tax on. The first three weeks the candidates called each other everything but A lady and A gentleman. From then on they just talked themselves out of votes. This great Old U. S. will move along just the same. Harry don't think so. But I do. If we have Elected the wrong man that is just another Blunder added to what we have had for twenty years. If congress is wrong, that is A national habit. Adlai just don't know how lucky he is. The U. S. has always got along without the help of Polotics; not help from them. All you could hear on the radios from Candidates was look at my record. Most of them records was like mine- -black and slimy. All they wanted was to do this public A service. Oh Yeah! They wanted A public job, so they could get their hand in the Public Pocket. I hope we have silence on Speeches and plenty of it. That old Elephant has got us, So let's get behind that man Ike and do A little cooperating. He shore will need it. Try to put as much in this Government as we take out. Act like we have A few brains, and not expect him to be A superman. It has took twenty years to get things in this mess and It will not be fixed in no month. Let Ike take care of the foreign countries. The United States will take care of itself.

NOVEMBER 20TH, 1952 . . .

Isenhower and His Cow Pasture Pool

Ike had better play all the cow pasture pool (golf) he wants to now. For shortly his days is going to be long and hard. They are already sniping at him. The best news that has come out of the D. C. lately is that Harry is wanting to take A trip around the world, but is short on cash. That is A common Disease with us all. He can surely borrow from R.F.C. And I might go his note. And put up the clip joint for security. He wants to take the trip and rest. He should be tired after getting us in the hole so far we will never get out. He will take A parting shot at Ike before he takes off I bet. Both barrels.

It seems like all the big shot Displaced democrats is going to write A book. They can't leave me at the post-I have wrote one too. Mine is about bucking horses, bronk riders and rop- ers (people). Theirs is educated Jargon, statesmen, Polotics and enterest hounds. Here in New Mexico Our Republican

Governor was elected again. That gives him two years more of Banquets and vacations. The people had A far away look in their eyes like A locoed steer. But the election has cured that. They hold their head up now like A new Tea Kettle Spout. and are smiling. A little weak yet, but it is there just the same, and will get better as time goes On.

There is A search warrant out for any democrat now, but like the old woman's biscuits at the hotel there ain't no more. This is all from doughBelly's Clip Joint, Taos. Better known as. the wall street of New Mexico.

Disease. is not catching. But most of that Bazzoo will subside like A bromo seltzer in A few days. Half of them will be in the class of the also run, and be like the little boy the bull butted--have no say coming. Then we can get The news of the korean war and how many has been killed on the football skirmish line. This is sure A funny world, but I sure like it. We are all suffering on account of too much comfort and don't know it.

NOVEMBER 27TH, 1952 . . .

doughBelly Has a Better Racket Than the Polotical Parisites

No more razzing the Polotical Parasites. I love every one of them. Why should I ruffle up my Bristles Because they have A better Racket than I have. Only they have to depend on the next election. My racket depends on how liberal I get with other peoples property. If they get caught being too liberal with the peoples money, they can resign. or have failing health (embezzlement). They called it stealing when I was convicted of the same thing.

Looks like Harry is going to gallop his mule around the world. And then Squat in Washington, D. C. AND THINK. He cannot get away from the Smell of polotics and start A breadline for the displaced Missouri poloticans. A non profit

Organization, shore. But it will pay Regardless of who is President, the man that carries the lunch pail will still tote the tax load. The big man can chisel, and does. That makes him A criminal. But listen at him scream when you tell him the truth. He has not heard it in A long time.

The revenue boys shore jumps plenty of twenty dollar bills looking for A nickel. But I honestly think Eisenhower will put heart in his work, and that will put confidence in the people. And there is nothing that will beat that old confidence. That is what we have been trying to buy overseas all the time and we have paid for confidence but it has not been delivered and won't be. Things is going all right. If A little mouse don't stampede the elephant. In short, too many hands on the steering wheel, and none on the brake pedal.

DECEMBER 11TH, 1952 . . .

The First Thanksgiving. And What It Done

Well, A few hundred years ago last week the pilgrims landed on the big pebble at Plymouth. Everybody knows that story. But what they don't know is that the first thanksgiving was A conference to see how many Indians they had killed and how much land had been took away from them. When the Boys landed on the big pebble there was no Taxes, no debts and the women done the work. Now look what has happened. As soon as they got their feet dry after the trip over here the work started--building churches, Court houses and institutions of insanity. To educate the People and now look what A mess we are in. we have got three tax consumers to every tax producer. Diplomats by the thousands. And none of them knows what to do. Bureaus By the Thousands-to tell you how to run your business. And outside of polotical business most of them don't know any more about the business they are trying to tell you how to run than A hog knows about Sunday. As they have spent most of their life going to some College learning how to make A living from the sweat of other people's brow. They have even got agencies to tell the Indians how to run their business. What the Indian needs is just what we all need-being let alone.

DECEMBER 25TH, 1952 . . .

Christmas Greetings. Try It.

JUST A LITTLE SMILE

Let's give something this Xmas that don't cost nothing. Not deductable from income. Something that will enrich the receiver, cost the giver nothing, and may be remembered A long time. And if used in great gobs will bring happiness at home. And make business as well as keep what you have. Bring rest to them that is tired and discouraged, and A ray of sunshine to them that is sad. Don't need no advertising. Everyone will notice it. Trouble cannot stand its presence. It can't be bought, begged, borrowed or stold. But don't try to keep it; for it is no good till it is give away. And if the person you give it to is too tired to give one in return, give him another shot-it don't cost nothing! And it will bring A ray of sunshine to this old war torn, weary world.

JUST A LITTLE SMILE

*Time marches on. and the old cowboy such as you see here is about gone. and they aint making no more.
branding chutes and barb Wire has robbed him of his heritage. the horns has been bred off of cattle. and spurs
off cowboys. the cattle has been give so many vitamins that the cow chips wont make A good fire no more.*

CHAPTER THREE

JANUARY 8TH, 1953 . . .

Just made A little tour to old Mexico. Viewed again the battleground--A gambling house-where me and three other thugs got throwed out in nineteen twenty-four. A light skirmish. And we lost. on our way back we stayed at the Paso Del Norte Hotel. One night--nine dollars. But we had Kleenex for toilet paper. Pretty soft for doughBelly. No?

Seen more cowboys than I ever seen in one gang before. No cattle but plenty of bull. Boots but not A speck of cow manure. Shined so bright that you could use them for A looking glass. And if them shiny things they had on their fingers was diamonds there was plenty of money represented there. But glass is reasonably cheap you know. And them boys don't talk thousands. They have read after Harry Truman so long they talk in millions.

JANUARY 22ND, 1953 . . .

Better Wait and See What Kid Isenhower Does Before Blowing Him Any Higher

There is not A doubt in my Simple mind, but what Ike Eisenhower is A great man. But I believe he has been blowed up about enough. Better wait and see how he gets along. He may be called everything But A lady and A gentleman before long. Such has happened before you know.

You hear them Screaming over the radio every day about the deaths on the highways. I give them the remedy for that several months ago. DON'T LET A CAR ON THE ROAD UNTIL IT IS PAID FOR--Nobody paid any attention to it. As long as there is fast high powered cars on the roads, there will be deaths. You can call out the army, the navy, and all the marines, legislate all the laws you can put on the books and machinery is still machinery and not perfect. This speed has become A costom and will be A costom as long as Fast cars is made. As many cars as there is on the roads today the death rate is not so great.

Before automobiles, if there had been as many horses and wagons on the road, there would have been one A day killed. I think the drivers of today is doing A good job. It is A wonder to me that there is not twenty-five killed in New Mexico Alone A day. As I see it the Nut behind the steering wheel is doing A good job. The Lawmaking body of New Mexico is ganged up in Santa Fe now to split the jackpot that was left over from the last raid on the taxpayers pocket book.

JANUARY 29TH, 1953 . . .

Isenhower Inaguaration. What a Mess

Wed. morning, January 21st. And the big brawl is over in Washington, D. C. and it took A million at the least to put it on and it will take another half million to clean away the rubbish. But we have A new man at the wheel--what we have needed for A long time. A clear head. A master mind. And someone that will give Commands firm and yet gentle. And inspire hope and confidence in the world. Without that there can be no peace.

We won't know till we see the outcome of the Wilson appointment whether country went Republican or General Motors. But that man Wilson has got to be smart to have as much money as he has with all them birds in the high bracket grabbing at his pocket book.

And the leader we have has got to have smart men. He can't do it all. He might have the wisdom of Solomon and the patience of Job, but that ain't enough. He has got to have help. And if he wants Wilson that is what he should have.

Ike needs the Nose of A Blood hound and the staying qualities of a bull dog. He will have to shake his head many more times than he nods it. I think. But who am I to think and what have I got to think with?

Exit Harry . . ..

The Difference Between Ike and Harry

It is not going to be funny this week. Just hard facts. That talk that Eisenhower made was wonderful. Ike and Harry is so much alike, yet such A vast different. Ike thinks hard and long before he speaks. Harry talked long and thought about what he had said three weeks later. It has been so long since The Great American public has heard A good man talk. It was sweet music to their sunburned ears.

There seems to be A brighter look in the eyes of the people. A new Note in the voice. It had got to where their noses was dragging in the dirt. Now it sticks up like the spout on A new coffee pot. Sure some of them didn't like the talk. They would kick if they was going to be hung with A new rope. He is going to turn Chang Shi check loose. Why make this war exclusive? If they want in the pot, deal them A hand. Even if the U. S. has to buy the chips. It looks like A game of freeze out anyhow. We will win the chips but who will cash them?

But look Ike is human and not A miracle. And he will need all the help and cooperation that can be given. We had better lay aside these petty larceny polotics and get on our feet. If Ike will take care of them foreigners. The United States will take care of itself. We have been doing that and we had all that static to buck in Washington.

Thank the Lord the old cows is still having calves and the sows pigs. The land is producing beans. We are not so bad off. Every Crisis has produced its man, so far. And it looks like that has been repeated in this crisis, too. Long may Ike Live and give us the leadership that we have needed for so long!!!

Poor Old George Washington

Washington's Birthday and wouldn't that old boy be surprised if he could walk out and see how things has been going since he cashed in. His equal rights to all and priveleges to none would be so funny and so silly that he would turn over in his grave so fast that you would think he was buried on A revolving door. With millions on welfare and social security the congressmen busy voting themselves pay raises, all the poloticans wanting to get on A pension for setting in one of them old hard chairs with cushion foam pads, guzzling groceries that the taxpayer paid for playing cow pasture pool (golf) to relieve the strain on the rear anatomy. George would not want them birds calling him pappy. Kids coming out of college thinking the four seasons of the year are baseball, basketball, football, and vacation. Spending more for Gymnasiums than we are on Professors. I am not as old as George but I don't savvy all I know about it. Teach the girls home Eck. and when they get their degree they can't cook A pan of cornbread. When they get married, the husband buys A can cutter and says "Honey, we are ready to keep house."

I am old fashioned, I believe in boarding in the kitchen, not in some tomain joint. Now, we get fat in war and thin in peace times. Everything is in reverse. If we was to go to climb A tree we would back up to it. The best of Scientific brains studying destruction, not construction. If you think this is funny you had better laugh now, for it is going to come to A sudden stop some day. We have got awful high, but we have got to come down.

I Am Going to Run for President

This atomic bomb seems to be too hot to hold and too dangerous to turn loose. You know that thing might just destroy the very thing that it was made to protect. And the H-bomb will make it look like Firing A blank. Man is getting so smart to kill A man with this guided missel. All you have to have is his address.

I believe I will run for President. After getting beat you can take A trip around the world, and the man that wins has to stay at home and play golf.

I wasted time to go to the Washington Story (moving Picture). Van Johnson had to take time out to kiss the leading woman. He can make kissing A woman sound like A cow pulling her foot out of A bog. And wall his eyes back like A dying calf in A hail storm. But he is getting along and I am selling real estate. He gets paid for doing it and I pay for seeing him do it so I guess he is smarter than I am.

The big boys in the senate went into A huddle the other day and come out and said things looked grim. Now they have woke up . . . I have knowed that for A long time, and didn't have to go into A huddle with anyone to find it out. But the poor things has so many social functions to attend that they don't have time to think and don't have too much to think with. If they would let farm prices alone. They will right themselves. Old supply and demand will take care of that if they will just let him alone. Oh Well they have got to have something to gripe about.

Death of Joe Stalin

Lots of people will read the obituary of Joe Stalin with A deep sigh of satisfaction. And lots of them same ones would do the same things as Joe did if they only had the chance. They don't stop to consider the times and conditions of bloodshed, hunger and misery that was his. The Russian kids of his day cut their teeth on A rifle Barrel. It has been and still is A survival of the fittest. And Joe survived to die A neutral death so he is not to be laughed at. He was brought up under Lenin, Marx and trotsky, demons in their own rights.

He learned all they could teach him and added what he knowed to that. Made him A smart man any way you look at him. He ruled millions with A iron hand and made them Like it. If they did not like it they said nothing. he didn't get what he knowed in class rooms or lecture halls and he out swapped and out managed men with degrees as long as A lariat rope. Tho we don't like what Joe did and his way of doing the things. Now that he is gone and can't fight back let's give him his just dues. He was smart and had the big savvy about how to handle people. It may and it may not be for the best that Joe Stalin is dead. Time alone will tell. It may mean A revolution in that country. As they elect over there by bullet, not ballot. Russia is as unpredictable as the wind, so let's hope for the best. But be prepared for the very worst if it should come.

MARCH 19TH, 1953 . . .

Friday, March the 13th and I had my income sentence read to me, not the first sentence I ever had. I have had sentences that it took 90 days and up to fill the order. Now, about them income taxes we hear so much about, here is my situation. I had A good T-bone steak last night and followed it with ice cream and strawberries, then went to the bank to borrow to pay my income tax and I am not screaming about Income Tax. I have seen the time when I had T-bone alright but I had to steal the beef, and that is no joke. I have all I want to eat, A good bed and A warm toilet. Now just what do I need with money? You can't eat it. Them one Dollar Bills would be hard chewing and them silver dollars would be hard to digest.

Chislers is what is hurting this country. They have more money than they could possibly spend sensible. And would give thousands to eat the supper I had last night and not suffer and then they squeal like A stuck hog about paying income. They think nothing about going to the night Club and paying One dollar A drink for algerian sheep dip (whiskey) and turn right around and try to chisel Sam out of the income. If them chislers were sent to Korea and made to pack ammunition to the boys on the firing line on their backs, eat Army chow and wiggle their ears and bray like A mule. For that chow, this chiseling would come to A sudden stop.

MAY 7TH, 1953 . . .

Peace and Contentment. Something We Smart Humans Dont Savvy

I was in cow country last Sunday to list A ranch. The one I have dreamed about but never expected to see. It has plenty of water and grass and A string of whitefaced cows laying in the shade of some trees. Some of the little calves sucking and wiggling their little tails to shoo the flys away. Them old fat cows was not worrying about Ike's golf score, tidelands oil, korean war, the income tax or how to chisel somebody out of something. Didn't have ulcers of the stomach or the hurry me to Jesus like we so-called humans.

I just wonder if we are smart. Oh sure we have the scientific brains, the atomic bomb, the jet planes, Preachers, teachers, Lawyers and Drs. Men with A string of letters behind their name as long as A lariet rope and they don't know what contentment is. Just as soon as they get their belly full, then they start trying to chisel somebody out of something. How they are going to gip Dear old Uncle Sam out of even A few dollars on income has become A national pass time. Everybody that has income is doing it (me too). The big dipos keeps giving us A shot in the arm about world peace. There can be no world peace till there is satisfaction and nobody is satisfied..Everybody wants everything and won't be satisfied with just A part of it. We are all living on the installment plan, paying last year's bills with this year's income and trying to act like big shots. And we have played the part of big shots so long we have begun to believe in all sincerity that we are big shots. And what A jolt it is going to be when we come out of this wonderful dream and have to face the facts. Dream on vain world. Rest in contentment you whitefaced cows. And we call this the age of enlightment!

MAY 21ST, 1953 . . .

Give Senator Joe McCarthy a One Way Ticket

I would like to make A little suggestion. Joe McCarthy wants to handle Foreign affairs so bad. Send him to Russia and let him envestigate Malenkove. He might find something that seems to be the bird that is gumming up the works. And now that Winston (Churchill) has on the Royal Garter he might make A good helper for Joe.

Another thing that I can't savvy is why there is so much ignorance in New Mexico and so many free Schools. I reckon these Lawyers here Can't even Count. Hurley and Chaves had to send to Washington to get Senators to fly down here to count the illegal votes. I just wonder if there is A hotel in Albuquerque good enough for them Boys. When the taxpayer is footing the bill. They should have to camp in some flop joint and be furnished A flit gun and A flash light so they could hunt bedbugs at night for pass time. Feed them New Mexico strawberries (Pinto Beans) for breakfast then they would have something to talk about when they got back to the District of Confusion.

May 28th, 1953 . . .

doughBelly Considering Running for Pres.

I want to be president of these U. S. I have everything it takes. I can hike the salary of the Reps. I can give away the tidelands. I can cut Taxes (SIC). I can order A gob of Atomic Cannons made that will be so big and heavy they will have to stay where they are made. The one thing I can't do is play that cowpasture pool (golf) . I never was A professor. I never wore one of them four cornered hats that looks like Washington crossing the Delaware. I never did give away A bank or have A bank account that was not in the red. What I would do. The first thing would be to kick the rear of McCarthy's britches to let him know that he is A very small part of this U. S. Tell these foreign countries that we can run our own business. Disband Congress. Send them birds home where they can fight with their wives and appropriate their own money and see how liberal they handle it. Declare A moratorium (boy that is A good word) on envestigations. Put A zipper on the lips of them that stayed in Washington and just let them take it off when they was eating. Have silence and plenty of it and our business would not be everybodys business and Russia wouldn't know before we do what we was going to do. I would try to do something for this country and I wouldn't ask England, France, and Japan's opinion to see if it suited them or not. And if they screamed too loud just chop off the groceries. We are feeding them and they want to tell us what to put on the table.

Fat Cows in Poor Country

I seen something the other day that was Beyond me. I seen A String of one thousand cattle on twenty to a hundred acres of land that the forest service people had planted in crested wheat grass. I run wild horses over that country twenty-five years ago and the land was so poor that you couldn't raise your voice above A whisper. But that grass is the salvation of that country. Them cattle was full of good grass and water and laying down in the shade. Contentment was everywhere.

There was some of the cows brothers that was just A little dissatisfied. It seemed I seen one that was looking for something to envestigate. I thought he looked like Senator McCarthy. But them bulls seemed to be getting along better than that many humans especially poloticans. They was not calling one another Subversives and other names. They was not getting ready for no coronation and seemed to be content to just let the world go along as long as they had that old water and grass and A full belly.

If it was not for elections and cornations and wars the human race might be happy too. But no we humans want everything that we don't need. The lust for power and the greed for gold is so strong in us that we ain't happy till we get it. The lust for power and the greed for gold is so strong in us that we ain't happy no time. Misery loves company and the human race has plenty of Company. We don't think only one way and that is to get more that we don't need and Can't use.

JUNE 11TH, 1953 . . .

Wonders Will Never Cease

I thought the days of Maricals was over but I changed my mind last Saturday. I was at the Espanola Valley Rodeo and seen A man jump at A steer Bulldogging. He jumped to the right but failed to clear his left foot from the stirrup. The horse jerked him loose from the steer and drug him two hundred feet kicking at him all the time. He was dragging right under the horses hind feet. Finally his boot come off and turned him loose. That man got up, went and got his boot. Another man brought his horse. He stepped up on him and rode back to the chutes. I had already said "there will be some slow driving and solemn singing. Another cowboy gone over the hill on A one way ticket." But he was not hurt at all. I done that same thing for A living for several years. Part of the time I lived and the other part I starved. But I got A little bit excited at the happening Sat. And I still say the Lord takes care of cowboys. But some of the time He has got to get in A hurry to stay with them. I have seen men killed most all ways in that game as well as hurt bad. But that took the cake. A man drug two hundred feet and the horse kicking at him all the time and get up and pull his boot on and ride off. Makes me still think A man is here for so long and then when the judge of time points his finger at him he is A dead stinking fish. I may be wrong as usual. But it looks that way to me. Anyway I got just A little bit excited and I am hard to excite. I played that game for fifteen years and can still walk and Talk. I am lucky. Just lucky!

JUNE 19TH, 1953 . . .

Long Live the Queen

I shore am glad that the coronation is over. Everything but the collection and cleaning up the rubbish. Long live the Queen and may all her troubles be little ones!

JUNE 29TH, 1953 . . .

I Dont Aim to Incriminate Myself. I Have Done That Before

I met A man the other day and he said to me very bluntly. doughBelly, you are just plain ignorant ain't you? I refused to answer that question for it might tend to incriminate me. That is what all the racketeers say. I am ignorant and don't deny it. The time has come that there is just one thing to be ashamed of-that is honesty. If you are honest you are poor and if you don't want people to believe what you tell them tell the truth. They won't believe you if they know it is true. This same man said I don't like the way you write. I said I don't like the way your hair is combed (for it was scrambled like spaghetti). He said you will never get nowhere. I said I don't want to get no where. I will tell you one thing Pard (he had been worth A lot of money). I am meeting A lot of you birds that think you are smart coming down the ladder and I am going up slowly but surely and as happy as A dead pig in the sunshine. I don't mister nobody. We are all just A womans child. I have been on the top and I have been on the bottom and I like the bottom best for I have more company. I write what I think and I don't care who it pleases or who it don't please. Blunt, frank and to the point and because it is blunt and to the point is the reason it is not going any better than it is. The American public just can't stand the truth anymore. It is too painful. I will be eating T-bones when plenty of the smart boys is eating chili and enjoying life in my simple way and that suits me. So why do they worry about me? I am not worrying about them. And I can smile at them and the knowledge they profess that they haven't got and the high and mighty thoughts they have.

Comedy That Cost Plenty. Congressional Record

I fell heir to A new Congressional Record and from reading that stretch of comedy I think our congressmen and Reps has Constipation of the brain and diaherria of the Mouth. One of them wanted to get A major league baseball set up in California-imagine that-A mansent to Washington drawing good money and he wishes to extend his remarks about A major league baseball set up.

If the Mr. president pro tempore and the whereases and be it resolved words was cut out there would just be nothing left. It don't seem like they learned to talk english. To read that congressional record sounds like to kids. One will say to the other. Let me chew your gum till recess and I will show you my sore toe. And everytime one of them gets up it is the same old stuff (S.O.S.) Mr. president--pro tempore--be it resolved that there is not enough to constitute A quorum. I move that this honorable body be recessed till next week.

I had Another letter wanting me to give money to something. This giving and guessing is getting to be A great grab. Give and guess who gets the money. The principal is all right but the interest is what hurts and most of it goes for interest. Bob Hope thinks he is funny and Red Skelton might make you smile but get the Congressional Record if you want to laugh out loud.

JULY 23RD, 1953 . . .

No Arguments Your Honor. Case Closed

I met A very entelligent looking man the other day and he whispered . . . doughBelly this is very confidential but I think you are crazy. I put my hand over my mouth and said . . . Pard I think you are right. He walked away looking back over his shoulder at me like A mule at A motherless colt. Now that is the way to stop A big argument. I just considered the source like the man the jackass kicked. And that is the way I look at this Matthews guy accusing some of the sky pilots of being one of them communist things. That accusation is one man's opinion. Why raise such A fuss about it? The papers is giving it A million dollars worth of publicity and it ain't worth A plugged nickel. If they will let Communism alone and not stir it so much it will not stink near so bad.

And this argument about burning the books. That is A wee bit silly. Has the people got to the point where they don't know what is good and what is bad? Can't they make their own decisions any more in this day of so-called Higher education? We are giving Moscow too much publicity. Seems like they are going to liquidate one of the big boys over there and listen to the polotical brass scream. That is nothing uncommon. It has been going on for years. One of our Big Scientists humped up and said that Russia had between two hundred and five hundred A-bombs. Anybody might guess that close. It don't look to me like he is so smart.

As long as this United States stays as it is-the best country in the world (with all its polotical twists)--there is nothing to fear. The big men in Washington Squall Wolf and it is just A harmless house cat. They want more advertising and that is A good way to get it.

There is nothing to get excited about till Congress puts birth control on the cows and sows. As long as there is calves horned and pigs coming into this world and A surplus of wheat. And the good mother earth grows beans and corn--we can have beans and corn bread and take care of our own business. We will get along.

A Lull Before the Big Stampede

Things is too quiet in the east. They have not killed a Primer this week. that I know of and they generally let me know when they are going to bump off one of them birds. It may be just A Lull before the big storm. like A herd of cattle They get very quiet before the big Stampede. Sing Munree is shore Throwing the Clamps on the Truce. One thing he has got them talking about it. But that is nothing uncommon. All them Dipos knows how to do is talk. The thing to do is Cut off the groceries of Sing. Let the hide on his belly get so slack that he can wipe his forehead with it and he will come to terms. Traveling expenses of the dipos going over there would balance the budget. But that would not be right as they would have to go somewhere else to get their money. Everyone of them has A different opinion. And I dont think any one of them birds knows any more than I do. And that is very little. I move that congress be Abolished. And the Traveling Dipos be kept at home and things might Straighten out. Stop printing the Congressional Record. put that money into comic books that can be understood by the children. The way it is nobody can savvy what it is all about. Too many be it resolved and wherebys and where ases. Just make it plain English. May the good Lord take care of the poloticians. The United States will take care of itself.

August 20th, 1953 . . .

The Old Cow Horse Was Smarter Than Both of Us

I was back up in cow country last Sunday that I rode over in 1923 under different conditions. In '23 I was looking a wall eyed bronk between the ears. Keeping A deep seat in the saddle to keep from being bucked off a long way from camp.

Sunday I had different ideas. I was trying to sell A man the ranch. Doing my very best to knock him loose from some of that green commodity called money but he wasn't so dumb. I turned on my line of bull and he looked at me like a mule at A motherless colt. as if to say you poor simp.

Funny but I knowed what he thought and I knowed he was right. But it was worth the trip to get back into cow country again. No telephones. No radios. But plenty of grass, water and contentment.

A good old Cow horse that I think had more brains than both of us so-called humans. He knowed what he was doing and was honest about it and we was both trying to do something to each other. Neither of us got the job done and the horse did. So I think he was smartest one of the bunch.

Seen some fat deer. But it won't be long till some of them will go down before the high powered rifle of hunters. Another example of the lust for blood that is predominant in the human race. And they call it Sport.

SEPTEMBER 3RD, 1953 . . .

Come Down Before We Get Knocked Down

I am not going to try to be funny this week. I am going to tell you just what I think. But that dont change things any. I could Be and I hope I am wrong. But I think we are heading into A nice little depression.

Not as bad as some I have seen but it will hurt A lot worse. for this reason. We have been living a Champagne Life on A beer salary. In short, living on the installment plan. AND WE HAVE GOT TO COME DOWN.

The old cowman is taking it on the chin. And Beef is the foundation of our living. And when you kick the foundation from under A house the house has got to fall.

And will some of the younger generation scream. About this administration. But this administration is doing all right. It is the American Public. Things has been give away, throwed and strawed till the time to stop has come. We have been buying what we wanted not what we needed. Never mind the price. The old installment plan has got us and we might just as well admit it. No use kidding ourselves.

The price that the farmer is getting for stuff. And the price the housewife has to pay for stuff has got too wide A space somewhere there is A leak. And A big one that has got to be plugged some way. We have just got to come down before somebody knocks us down. and we had just as well get used to the idea now and it won't hurt so bad later on. Dont scream about taxes as long as you have the groceries.

SEPTEMBER 10TH, 1953 . . .

I was to have went to Texas to Judge A bronk riding contest over labor day. But they stopped my pay and I got mad and I aint going. They said all they could give me was the honor. Now that is poor eating unless you have lots of cream and sugar to spread over it. I would have to drive My jeep station wagon. and among them Cadillacs it would be like A motherless calf at A round up. Some people might think one of them Cads had had A colt. ·

Well anyway I bet they have the show just the same. Of course it will not be as Good as if I had of been there and told them how as I am A very Smart little man.

SEPTEMBER 17TH, 1953 . . .

Poor Kinsey

Dr. Kinsey investigated five thousand women and every paper in the country had screaming headlines about it. Then some women took A notion to take A cross section review of Dr. Kinsey. What they found out--NO comment-They must have looked above the collar line because you sure won't find anything there.

Harry Truman, the Admiral of the Missouri Navy, came out of the bushes long enough to take A potshot at Ike and his administration. He forgot it took him eight years to give A first mortgage on the whole U. S. and he thinks Ike should pay off that mortgage in eight months and improve his golf at the same time. Harry sure did pour off his obnoxious gas but it didn't amount to anything. Its that synthetic gas-too thick to burn and too thin to stick. It kept rolling back on him all the time.

Truman stevenson and the other big shots of the democratic party is meeting soon to take A potshot at Ike in the big off year convention. They are sure oiling up the guns.

The U. S. told the Korean boys to deliver all the POW's or else. Else what? Wau lung chung will do just as he pleases. He has done that all the time and what can they do about it. They might get him up before that Senate Crime Committee but he would refuse to answer questions on the grounds that It might tend to incriminate him.

September 24th, 1953 . . .

The Enjoyment of Being Insane

I was over at the La Mesa race meet sunday. And I beheld insanity in all its glory. The violently insane of the Las Vegas asylum would have showed up in entelligence like a red vest on A fat man compared to some of the socalled smart ones there. They was trying to beat the old Par Mutiel machine out of that green commodity called money. They had pouches under their eyes and protruding Bellys. And A craze for money. And nerves as tight as A fiddle string. The thorobred horses was the most sensible thing I saw and they was nervous. I seen people there losing money that would not give A dime to seen the statue of liberty bow down and take a drink of water. And they talk about stopping gambling. What A joke?

(80)

One woman I took notice of was seventy years old I think. Gambling with both hands and whiffing uptown cigarettes through her holler head. Lighting one from the butt of the other and stomping around like A bull in A china closet. I shore had fun!

For making money I would rather have them Par mutiels than the US mint. The Suckers was coming in herds plunking down the money. Losing and then shake their heads, cuss and go again.

Funny little old world But I shore love it. I reckon I am too old and too dumb to see the funny side of that stuff. Never had money to know what it is good for. But as long as I have what I have got now. Three meals A day, A soft bed and Warm toilet and not handcuffed so I can wander around and watch such things done by the socalled smart people. See the par mutiels reduce the pocket book. Drive a jeep. Not a cad. At the high speed of forty miles an hour. If I want to get there sooner start quicker. Life will continue to be one great round of pleasure.

OCTOBER 8TH, 1953 . . .

Flying Low in a Buick

Last Sat I boarded A single engine Buick car and took off swift and silent like the smoke from hot water with two pilots. With A heavy foot on the Gas pedal. They set that buick down in texas the next morning after circling the field A few times at Nocona where I rode bucking horses some forty years ago with A wild west show. And what A change! All you can see there now is oil and gas. It was A cow country when I first seen it. Cattle there yet But they are A by-product.

When you stepped outside of them Cold air fumigated houses the heat would burn the hair out of your nose. I drank so much water that my belly thought my throat was taking in washing.

(81)

Let them boys have the money. And the oil. But just give me Northern New Mexico and the climate we have And what groceries I can devour. And the satisfaction of watching the world go nuts. This may be the land of Manyanna and Come ala Vou. Where they call women Muhares and corn mice. Mosquitoes hay hands and dogs payrolls. But it shore suits me. Because I don't know any better and I am too smart to be educated now I reckon.

I was the tail gunner in that buick. All I had to do was look, But the only thing I seen was the road ahead, wondering if they was going to make the next curve or go straight on.

I had a nice time. Met some good people and one Newspaper man but Taos shore looked good to me when we got back in sight of it. When I walked into the house the wife hollered at me from the bedroom and said is that you dough? I got the first long breath I had had for three days and said I think so but I am not sure.

OCTOBER 15TH, 1953 . . .

The Ball Game Is Over

Well I am shore glad that the world serious ball games is over. The Yankees won. That has got to be A habit almost as shore as taxes. Anyway the radios had something on besides the Chaves Hurley squak.

The boys ranch drive is on to raise sixty five million A few Hundred thousand to make good Citizens out of the boys. I have A remedy for making Good Citizens out of them. Learn them to do something besides loaf and above all stay out of polotics. Get A civil service job. Get on social security and wait for the old age Pension. When they get married buy A can cutter and say Honey we are ready to start housekeeping. Dont eat at home. Dine out where there is good atmosphere. Dont mind the chuck. It is the atmosphere that counts. Get a college dip. Get A job selling second hand cars or keep books for the old Womans hogzillary and be A non-producing Citizen. That is what 90 percent of us is now.

I got a new membership Roster of the New Mexico realtors. It says I quote. whatsoever ye would that men should do unto you, do you also unto them, end quote. And I will add. Do it first. As that is what we are all doing anyway. Never mind ethics. Get the money.

OCTOBER 22ND, 1953 . . .

Gamblers and Bee Girls

Its against the law to gamble in New Mexico. But the Par Mutel machines shore made A string of criminals this year. The people shot almost eight million Dollars through the machines at the three race meets. It is against the law to bet (This machine betting was called WAGERING) on a Dice game or roulette wheel That is A game of chance. By the time the dee ducts got done the difference between Wagering and Gambling is A Technicality (that is A little bug that gets under the hide of justice and gives justice the blind staggers).

I just wonder why gambling is not legalized. Oh shore there would be people running around in circles. There would be wailing and knocking out of teeth over losing money on the dice game. But this other dont count. And too there would be mean gamblers and Bee girls-Horrible creatures.

I worked in las Vegas nevada five months and did not get raped one time. Never dodged a Bullet. And I have not got A knife scar to show for being there. And I never had my arm twisted by one of them Bee girls Them gamblers and Bee girls is human and attend strictly to their own business. Some of them Bee girls is good to look at as their Differential sticks out like A rocky mountain pumpkin. I seen Gambling at Las Vegas Nevada at the top in war time. And it is the cleanest run business I have ever seen. No polotics there. You take care of your business and let the other fellows alone.

(83)

Now this eight million that was gambled in N. M. No matter what you call it, It is gambling And the ones that done it broke the law. And the Judges, Lawyers and Drs., Preachers and Teachers was at the races. The small fry when they had the money. Woe unto you Hypocrites that made Gambling a crime.

OCTOBER 29TH, 1953 . . .

Another Cornvention

I am taking off Sunday for another one of them State Real Estate Cornventions at Carlsbad. I will have to eat some of them old Banquets, set at A table and use A knife and fork. We are having the Annual Meeting to split this years Jack pot and arrange to rob the public for another year. It is A great Racket and I shore love it.

But I will say this Nowdays if you havent got A racket you are behind the eight ball and Liable to stay there, for if you get out and work I mean work. You will scratch the head of A poor man all the days of your Life For when you work and live and the Dee ducks get done with the pay check you have the Receipt for social security left and that is about all.

And at the convention I will have to listen to some of them Speakers talk about how to sell real Estate that I bet dident buy their own home. There will be pamphlets to tell you how to sell the stuff. But I don't think them little Booklets is any good.

The thing to do in selling A man something that he can't pay for is to get him so up in the air that he dont know just what he is doing And when he gets that far away look in his eyes like A locoed steer that Is The time to have him sign right there telling him all the time me and my Lawyer will do the rest. We will.

When we get done with commissions, Legal Fees, abstracts, Opinions of title, transaction taxes and other Messilanious articles too numerous to mention, The buyer is in debt the rest of his life. And the seller is A good man but he just used bad judgment as the Real Estate Broker and the legal Profession has the money. But the racket is legitimate and there is nothing you can do about it.

November 5th, 1953 . . .

The Gentleman From Chicago Will Now Take the Floor

Well the Real Estate convention was A grand success. I guess. I Heard A gob of them smart men talk. And I am just as bad Confused as I was. One would tell you that there was bad times coming. I knowed that. The other one would get up and say that there was going to be no more hard times. I doubt that.

I went to the country club, and set through one of them Banquets. And after it was over A big Bull shipper from Chicago arose, walled his eyes back like A dying calf in A hail storm, and let off A blast of obnoxious gas. It was all right but he could have quit sooner and it would have been better.

I done no spouting off. As there is one thing I have Learned in my Old age is that you can learn more Listening than you can Talking. Another thing I learned was that the big men is just guessing at what times ahead is going to be. And I can guess too. And I think my guess is Just as good as theirs. And I am going to do the very best I know how and they will do the same. If things come my way fine and if they dont that will have to be fine too.

There was talks about how to sell real Estate. There is no set rules for that. Each client that walks in the door is another human. and each one is different. Just like finger prints. I look each one over and try to guess what line of bull will suit the best. Start on that line and if it dont look like it is taking I will stop that one and start on A different line.

Be ready to switch Decks at any time if the deal is going against you. And if you have to slip in A cold deck dont get caught.

Horse Sense

I was around horses so long that some of that common horse sense had to rub off on me. And that same common horse sense tells me that what is wrong with this great United States today is Too Much scientific bunk. And not enough common sense. All we hear today is more and higher education. When this great country was run by cowmen, Lumber men and miners We dident owe nobody anything. Since the legal profession and the Diplomats has took over we are even with the world. We owe as many as we dont owe.

Our Vice President is on A good will tour around the world. trying to show the other boys how smart we are. He had better be at home. They already know how little we know. Russia is called illiterate. But they have got our socalled smart diplomats turning hand springs like A turpintined cat. We dont know where we are going and wont know when we get there.

When our State and National law makers meet they spend their time wrangling over how much they will raise their own salary. and Voting pensions to run down dissipated poloticians. That has never produced but two things--Misery and Confusion.

Our colleges is teaching football, baseball, basket ball and vacation. We try to give our child A better education. So he will not have to work and will be better qualified to cheat the other ones of his time out of what belongs to them. It is all right to give our kids A chance But not A cinch.

Our scientists is working day and night on emplements of destruction Not Construction. Every baby barned today comes into the world with A mortgage clause wrote across the first diaper he wears. But we have to pay the fiddler if we want to dance. And we are all dancing.

DECEMBER 3RD, 1953 ...

Truman on White and Brownell

Say this Dexter White, Junior Brownell, Harry Truman and Joe McCarthy has shore got one little man by the name of doughBelly messed up. The more I read and listen to it the Less I know and believe. Harry says that it is demagogary (whatever that is) But it sounds A little like polotics to me. A polotican has got to go pretty low to come up. And most of them never get up.

I was in Santa Fe A few days ago. Trying to borrow money (No dice on that) But I did learn A new word. AGENDA. And it was being knocked around the State Capitol like A motherless calf at A round up. Every time you asked somebody Something they had to look at the AGENDA. The time is coming when them people around the State Capitol will not talk English it will be that latin. gibberish. I am going to fix me one of them AGENDAS.

Since that bird that has the C.P.A. behind his name and does his very best to keep me out of jail (and he may fail this time) bounced into my Clip Joint the other day and gave me an estimate on my income. He was very blunt; dident lick his lips or button his coat. It would have been more but he ran out of figures I guess.

I am A busy little man trying to get the bank paid up and build up their confidence in me so I can borrow the money to pay the man with the whiskers. After I pay the bank back I can start trying to make A living. So life is one continual round of pleasure.

This is thanksgiving. and I can be thankful that the bankers is dumb enough to loan me the money to pay income (if they Do) so I can go on fleecing the public just like many others do. but it is legitimate I hope. and if it aint it wont be the first business I ever had that was not legitimate. And maybe not the last.

DECEMBER 10TH, 1953 . . .

Mac Is Punch Drunk

You know I think that man McCarthy is just A little punch drunk. he has had so many fights and has never won one But I can sympathize with him. That is my shape. But I do know enough to quit. And he just keeps on. If he was going to be hung with a new rope he would want to envestigate the man that made the rope. and it seems like some of the boys is afraid of him. It all sums up to the same old thing--POLOTICS and votes.

I am going to start A manufacturing plant and make Tags to go on the many men that is going to run for Governor. I seen one of them and he dont look so hot to me. I have made A resolve. That in this next election I am not going to vote for what A man is. I am going to vote for what he aint.

The Bird that has got LLDs, BVDs and B.S. degrees hung all over him. It is just impossible for him to have any good hard Gray matter in his noggin. He has been in too many Schools and Colleges. He looks like A oil and gas man to me. And we have had enough of them kind. They can shore play Banquets and shake hands with A strong grip. But when it comes to making a decision they have to look for A precedent. and the way things is now there just aint no more of them Precedents.

ike is getting panned some. but I am still with him. and he is still going about his business just like he did when he spanked the pants of the Germans. aint looking back for wood, water or coal. Harry and the boys spout off about him. But he is just like the man the jackass kicked. just considers the source and goes on. Stay right in there Ike. I am with you.

(88)

DECEMBER 17TH) 1953 . . .

Number 0114421

If you run A business or have A business to run you, you have got to be up in society. have A bookkeeper, A lawyer and A stenographer. The bookeeper to keep you posted on how much income to pay. The Lawyer to get you out of jail if you dont pay, the steno. to write you while you are in jail.

I had A letter from the U.S. Treasury Dept. U.S. Court House, Albuquerque. Number 0114421. It says do not staple, fold or mutilate (whatever that is). I thought my dear old uncle was sending me A check when I looked at that string of figures. But now I think it will be my number when I get to the big house at Leavensworth. I done ninety days by order of A federal Judge. But the ink was not dry till that time was done.

This will be different. A long restful vacation. for I dont have the money to hire A good mouthpiece. This seems to be about survivor insurance. in social security or something. It looks like they think I will not survive to spend my social security.

What I am trying to point out is. if your business will not support A bookkeeper, A lawyer, and A stenographer, close the business. Get a close relative in some big office so you can get on relief and live happy ever after.

I am handling that little pink piece of pasteboard with gloves on to keep from leaving fingerprints. The F.B.I. has one set of them and I dont want to clutter up the files with another set. I am going to take it to my bookeeper. If he dont know what to do I will then see my ATTORNEY. An if he shakes his head I will call the U. S. Marshal and give up. for there is no use to run. They are like the undertaking business. They will nail you in the end.

The Fickle Finger of Destiny

The time for peace on earth, Good will toward men is here. That angel that brought the Great Messiah to earth passed over the homes of the rich and mighty and deposited the Great Baby in A manger. But the fickle finger of destiny points any way but to peace on earth. The north koreans don't want peace for they are not whipped. When a man is thrashed out good he will not argue about stopping the fight.

Our great leaders is confused. torn between the destructiveness of the atomic bomb and the powerful voting ballot. One can blow them out of office. The other can blow them off the face of the earth. Both have to be considered it looks like. No two has the same view.

Our president is doing the best he can with the tools he has to work with, which is many and varied. He is going to have to have the wisdom of Solomon and the Patience of Job to weather the storm. For 1954 is going to be stormy. As the dark war clouds gather lets give him our support, regardless of what you believe polotically.

What if it does take all you have made to pay the income tax. You are still living in the greatest country in the world. If you dont like the country get your dirty socks and tooth brush and move.

Try to put as much in this great Government as you take out. If you have made enough money to pay income think how lucky you are. and the many millions that has not been so lucky.

And dont say Oh it was my brains. You might think you are the master of your ship. NUTS! You are not even a deck hand on A river Scow. The old hand of destiny is over you all the time guiding your every move. And the few paltry dollars you have was made from the sweat of some one elses brow. Meet your fellow man, Give them A smile. It dont cost nothing. Don't think you are so high and mightly. The great Babe of Bethlehem was barned in A manger.

DECEMBER 31ST, 1953 . . .

The New Baby Is Borned

As 1953 does the houdini disappearing act we wonder what '54 will bring. The only thing that is sure of is an off-year election. More bitter name calling and mud slinging. The fifty four baby will have A first mortgage emblazoned across the seat of his first diaper, and A halo of mystery on his head.

What is in store for us in fifty four is anybody's guess. The farmers and ranchers (the backbone of it all) has graduated from A cow horse to A cadallic.. Got A masters degree in luxury and ease. and even with the world owe as many as they dont owe. living A champagning life on A beer income.

And the beer income is from oil. Something that you cant eat or drink. worshipping at the shrine of E pluribus unium and prostituting the natural resources of the land for things that he has no use for. We have the atomic Bomb and dont know what to do with it.

The Atomic baby that was barned at the white sands proving ground looked like a baby of deliverance. And now it has turned into A night mare. to hot to hold and to dangerous to turn loose. And it is called the age of enlightment. I wonder--

A good old white faced cow will eat, drink and lay down contented. But we so-called smart humans eat, drink and start looking for some one that we can beat out of something.

A long eared mule wont eat too much or drink too much. We humans will do both and then cry about a hangover and scream for a pill shooter. But we cant back up. It is too late now. We have got to go and see what the final finish will be. At the end of '54 we may still be stumbling in the dark but let's hope not. As long as congress dont put birth control on cattle and Hogs we will make it.

I know just how he feels and just what he is saying but it wont go through the mails in print. new boots. Bucked off A long ways from camp. carrying the boot that hurt the worst. oh for that six shooter that is tied on the saddle.

Chapter Four

Joe McCarthy, U. S. doughBelly

Well, Fifty three has gone into the discards. Many this morning will come to with A Hangover and as soon as they are able will start singing the Income Tax blues. Income will go down and social security up. One will take care of the other.

The scientific world has made wonderful progress in '53. (atomic) They have found ways to kill more people faster and with less pain. Jet planes that you can kill A man and get away so fast you cant hear him Squawk. Faster automobiles and more slaughtering on the highways. If they will stop installments, highway deaths will stop. It is the nut behind the steering wheel that causes most of them.

Ike is going to deliver his message of the State of the Nation. He will talk for some time. I could say it in A very few words. It is in A helluva state! I am so smart I dont see how they get along in Washington without me. But they have Joe McCarthy.

I got A tubful of Christmas cards. One man wrote that he wanted to live to see the day when My name would be A byline in every newspaper. He is nuts! Or going to be A candidate for something. Many said things that I cannot get through the mail but they must be reading my stuff. And that is what counts. I am not making any money out of this writing but I am shore having fun. Exit '53. Welcome '54 and may you bring A little satisfaction and plenty of peace on earth, Good Will to men to this war-torn, weary world.

Kangaroo Court Was Called to Order

Well some old joker pounded the gavel and the eighty third congress went into action to muddle up the affairs of the U. S. For A spell. but the first day dident last long. Only twenty-five minutes. And they retired to fight the battle in the cocktail lounge. Ike told them what he wanted in his state of the nation talk. but he had that too early in the mqrning. Most of the boys was there. I hope. But they was not awake yet. Had not partook of their orange juice. and morning shot of the algerian sheep dip.

Most of them senators and Reps. Have been admitted to the bar (and ordered Scotch and Soda). What A gathering of the legal profession! They shore are going to throw Ike some fast Curves. But he is in there catching. And he aint the rank amature now that he was when he took that job. He dont fall for that old confidence stuff as easy as he did.

January 28th, 1954 ...

Begin the Free Feeds

I started last night on A round of Banquets that will last A week nearly. And if my little protruding belly stands the strain of four of them Banquets I am going to run for governor of New Mexico. for all they have to do is attend banquets and guzzle in the surplus groceries.

That was A fancy one last night. You ordered what you wanted. The female of the specie was A cute little thing. She dashed up to me and asked what I would have. I said Oh just bring me anything the other boys wont eat. She looked at me like A mule at A motherless colt. they had A table loaded with them cheese and shrimp that was all curled up like they had died with the cramps and they was harpooned with A tooth pick.

I watched the woman in front of me and she soused one of them cramped up shrimp into A bowl of something red so did I and it went down the hatch and did not come back so I guess it was all right. They would be easier to take in A capsule.

I am to be guest speaker at something in Albuquerque next Monday. I guess they will give me A whole brick building one brick at A time. But they asked for it. But I bet they never ask for it no more. Then I will come home and try to get better. I know I will never get well.

FEBRUARY 4TH, 1954 . . .

After Dinner I Spout Off

Got home last night from A round of Banquets (two in one day) broke Tired and Constipated. If my little belly stands the strain of all them Banquets I am going to run for governor. They fed us Chicken at two of them feeds. You may not know it but they never kill A rooster in new Mexico till he loses his first race with A hen.

I was the bloke speiler (Guest Speaker) at the one in Albuquerque. The crowd seemed to be made of Lawyers and Real Estate Racketeers and looked to be as good A gang of Histers as ever put powder in A safe. I loomed up among them dressed up birds like A red vest on A fat man. but with my broad shoulders, big hands and protruding belly I got along fine. All was sober, and there was not A dish chunked my way. Must have been good people.

And the lawyer that introduced me as could be expected he handled the truth with gloves on afraid he might leave finger prints. said very little as he introduced me. He had very little to talk about.

I went from there to Station K.O.B. and was showed through that place. That was some joint: that is the place we hear all the squealing sopranos and Johnny Gs bread and

Barkers Jeeps. The jeep part is all right (I am wearing out my second one now) But that bread. He ort to have A good old sourdough biscuit after the sour dough begins to turn green. Then he would know what bread is.

It was A nice trip and I met some very nice people. At least they was nice to me. It might have been sympathy. but I dident know the difference. So what?

FEBRUARY 11TH, 1954 . . .

Polotical Cornvention

Hear ye! Hear ye! The polotical cornventions is now coming to order. The repubs will meet in Santa Fe the last of this month. And I am going to make A motion that Senator McCarthy come down and envestigate the men in town and of Course that means that Dr. Kinsey will have to envestigate the women. to see that none of the Deligates becomes contaminated with the Democratic Plague.

The Democrats is going first class. They are going to Albuquerque to have their palaver and split the jack pot. The demos have Simms wrinkle and wise and one or two other rounders. And they will all tell you that they are in the race for the good of the dear old sunshine State. DONT swaller that old line of bull. They are there for what they can get.

The dear old G.O.P. is after the same thing. and that thing has on it In God We Trust, There is not A one of them that will not spend more trying to get the Governor's office than it will pay. You guess the rest, polotics income tax and social security has got us by the seat of the britches and A downhill drag. and there is nothing we can do about it. They are like the undertaking business. They will nail you in the end. just like A bull in A china closet. What they cant mess up they will tramp on.

I am satisfied till they try to put birth control on cows and sows and then I am going to raise my bristles. as it is

I am just setting back watching the world go nuts. The rat race is on. and we will have polotics for breakfast dinner and supper for the next ten months. Oh well we like it . . .

The Same Deck Shuffled and Cut

Well if you dont think I am getting up in society listen. I have had two of the pin headed pollticans in to see me lately. Both running just as hard as they can but not getting there fast enough. I am afraid. One wants to be state corporation commissioner. Terrible Terry Moynihan. He dont know much or he would not want the job. has all he can. or will do at home. But he has that far away look in his eyes. like A locoed sheep. and he is living on polotics (he might not last long). The other one wants to be supreme court something. about law way high up. Well I might go for him. I will never have enough to get A case that high in court anyway. so he will not bother me any.

But to be honest (which I aint very often) as I see it. After the election it will be the same old deck. that has only been reshuffled. The same cards but in A different location. as it has been since I started listening to poloticans. The same old line of Bull. Honest (when they think it will pay off) Reliable (dont lay to much money on that bet. you might lose). No partiality shown (unless for A fee) Sober (if the bartenders goes on A set down strike) not trying to get the office for any financial gain. (Tie your little Bull outside). It will no doubt cost the man that is elected Gov. fifty thousand. and the salary in two years is thirty thousand. And there never has been A governor come out of office and go on relief. So you make A guess. I have done made mine.

I am in favor of electing Bob Hope to the united States Congress. He is getting about silly enough to make A good congressman.

Move the State Capitol

Say these would be office seekers is shore busy now days. They all have good seats but want some place to put them. Most of them in the governors chair or the Corporation commission. as gov. they have to attend them old banquets and stuff the belly. That corporation com. job I dont savvy just what there is so great about that. For dem gov. there is wrinkle wise and simms and others too numerous to mention. Wise seems to have the broadest seat. and it may be A little too broad. Shep started A little late in his race for commissioner but he is closing in fast. Terrible Terry Moynihan from Taos has wore out two automobiles and A jeep already and has got two votes in the bag (maybe). Most of these poloticians can come up in the public's eye.

Our boy Ike is in Cal. engaged in another game of cow pasture pool (golf) and resting. I just dont know how them boys ever gets time to work. They are so busy resting.

The best thing I can see to do about this polotical situation is abolish the State house and all that goes with it and move the whole she bang over to the State Pententeary. to the warden and his boys. 'Then things would straighten out. They know what the score is and they stay at the same place most of the time. There would be no trouble catching them at home. Kick out about ninety per cent of the laws we have and put the other ten percent to work. on everybody not just them that has got no money. and nationally stop the good will tours. Keep the diplomats at home and pay off the National debt in A wee bit of time.

I Am Grandpap

I have just got done being A deligate to the county polotics convention and I heard two of the leaders of the young Demos talk and after they got done the chairman of the cornvention had to say something so he up and says they are the leaders of tomorrow. If that is the case I shore dont know where we are going.

Here is most of the talk but it took some time to get it all out. Ladies and gentlemen and fellow democrats (they had to tell most of us what we was) we are here to fight our common enemy the Republican party. We have lost the control of the Great State of New Mexico for four years BECAUSE, we have not had Harmony in the party.

One of them guys drank so much water while he was talking that I bet his belly thought his throat was taking in washings. and he was as nervous as A bowl of Jello. his lips must have been awful dry. he kept licking them all the time. and he had A very hard time getting his coat buttoned right. They was something about the young demos and Lawyers on top of that. Now if that aint A combination. But this was just the preliminary. I am going to the main bout in Albuquerque. That is the place that I will hear the best of the expert liars. No Marquis of Queensberry rules there. it will be gouge, scratch, kick and bite and promise everything but what they are going to do if elected. A honest man would loom up at that shindig like A outhouse in a fog. My next report if I survive the main bout will be from

Los Angeles where I am going to see my new and only Grandchild. Here I am Grandfather. Who said time marches on? I dont have to be reminded of that.

Nervous Teardown

Back in Dear old Taos . . . and every time I leave here and go some other place I think more of New Mexico.

That weather in Cal you could slice it with A dull knife. there is too many houses for you to see the country. If you go fast you run over something. if you dont go fast something runs over you. Things is just too fast for a country boy.

The new grand child cried so I decided that it had advanced far enough from the stages of evolution to keep.

I took A car ride with my other girl (Kathleen) and almost had one of them Nervous tear downs before we got back to her home. Traffic scrambled like Spaghetti and everybody trying to run over somebody else.

I seen Hollywood that is the place where you go to bed with A beautiful dream and wake up with A night mare. There is some beautiful angels out there but they have arms not wings. but with planes roaring over head, Ambulances and police sirens screaming on the ground, about five days was all I could stand.

We took A plane and before I had time to look the hostess over and get the seat warm we was there. I wanted to spank the hostess. She was A pretty thing to look at. But the wife objected. Objection sustained as the man of the legal profession says.

All in all it was a wonderful trip but just give me good old New Mexico. with all its faults. The people is still friendly and they have not got enough money to get their nose up in the air yet like A new coffee pot spout. and I can live and let the world go by. Let me live in A house in the mountains and be a friend of man. where there is little of the sham and shallow pretence.

Fast Automobiles

The screaming goes on about the highway deaths Our law makers and diplomats go at that as usual BACKWARDS. As long as they make automobiles that has two hundred horsepower and will cruise at A hundred miles an hour. And Nuts behind the steering wheel that has nothing above the collar line but salty water and sawdust. deaths on the road will not stop.

I give the remedy sometime back. DONT LET A CAR ON THE ROAD TILL IT IS PAID FOR. That will save plenty of money. No highway patrolmen. no highway maintenance no need for better roads, and the highways can be planted in beans.

My jeep has ninety horse power and will make fifty five miles an hour under A full head of steam. and I have never started anywhere yet that I have not got there. If I want to get there quicker I just start earlier.

There is just no ARGUMENT. we are moving too fast. everybody is in A big hurry to get some place. dont know where they are going and many dont when they get there. with luthimatic take off, hydramatic come back, power shift and nothing to do but set and whiff uptown cigarettes through their hollow heads. It is A wonder there is not more deaths than there is.   ·

When they quit trying to make jet planes out of automobiles, cut the speed limit to sixty miles an hour, and that means to all people (EVERYBODY) not to just A chosen few, the highway accidents will slow down and the roads be safe to drive on.

Give McCarthy What Paddy Give the

Some of them big men in Washington should kick the seat of that man McCarthy's britches so fast he would think they was patting for him to dance. he wants everything envestigated. But McCarthy. And who is going to envestigate the envestigator?

Now the way I get it there is about Twenty thousand active Communists in the whole U. S. That is about one in A thousand. Now if 999 good old reliable American people cant watch one lousy rat we had better go into A hole and pull the hole in after us.

Go on Mac do your envestigating. never mind the boys over seas that want to come home. don't mention indo-china that will not get your name in the headlines or your mug on T. V. You might be A great leader but I shore don't want to follow you.

APRIL 8TH, 1954 . . .

We Need More Human Relations

I like to look back for you can see farther looking back than you can looking forward. There is A few bright spots in looking back that will afford you A little chuckle when there was no McCarthy envestigations. when man had A little confidence in mankind. when you met your neighbor he would not look at you out of the corner of his eye like A mule at A motherless colt. Confidence now days is like the old womans biscuits at the hotel. there hain't no more.

Now days if you are in polotics you have to be a crook and A grafter. if not in polotics you are an undesirable citizen and subject to deportation. If you go to church and pay the preacher you are A hypocrite. If you dont you are A sinner and A tightwad. No wonder people have ulcers.

I know I am A smart man (ask doughBelly. he knows

everything. NEARLY) but this has got me stopped. what are they going to do with the atomic bomb? when are we going to hear the last of the election FRAUD?

We live in better houses. we drive big powerful automobiles. we get where we are going quicker and kill ourselves faster. But the big question in my weak mind is are we happy. The United Nations is trying to work out A plan for world peace and there can be no world peace until there is satisfaction.

APRIL 22ND, 1954 . . .

If You Dont Like It Don't Read It

I have decided fully that if I had any sense I would go crazy. I read some of the simple things that is published in magazines and papers. that is not so wrapped up in pig latin and nonesense that only the over-educated half wits can savvy.

I read where two men in Texas paid one hundred thousand dollars for Half enterest in one bull. Some BULL. and what will his calves be good for. MANURE.

Our great senators and Reps. throw out two hundred thousand dollars for the New Mexico election fraud envestigation. Results boiled down. ZERO. Surplus food of all kinds stored that is rotting. and miners in several States going hungry. and it would take two months for some attorney General to find out if it was legal to give it to them. and the attorney that has to give that decision never done nothing but go to School. and he studied latin and nonsense. and got A degree in nonesense.

The old common cowman that made this country great is as out of date as A model A ford.

One of the big senators of this country is letting his greed for power and lust for gold take the lead over welfare of the country. Some people might not like what I say. I DONT CARE, savvy? If you dont like it dont read it.

(103)

Uneasy Payments

Things is so quiet here in New Mexico that you can hear the notes fall due at the bank. I got one of them OD's today and that don't mean officer of the Day either.

the wanting to be public office holders is all that is making an fuss at all. they are as busy as An old hen with one Chicken. When you meet one of them he has A grin like A wave on A slop bucket but that is for your vote not because he likes you.

I owe the federal Government I owe the state I owe the bank. I am even with the world, I owe as many as I dont owe. I am letting them do the worrying.

What has happened to Harry Truman? He has not let out a peep in weeks . . . Must be busy plowing his corn. and the only way to break his silence is for some one to say his daughter cant sing.

Indo China is getting hot. There is going to be some very important decisions to make before long. The Congress will adjourn and Ike will have to play some more cow pasture pool (golf).

They cant find A man honest enough in Washington to cross swords with that Napoleon of the U. S. Senator JOE McCARTHY. He shore has got them all on the lam. When he says rabbit they shore start hopping.

These uneasy payments on Cars and Television sets has took everything the boys has in their pockets. Them payments will get the pockets next. Well such is life. we have been living A champagne life on A beer salary. most of that on paper. but We Have got to come down.

Roping Contest

I had the pleasure of watching something walk around last Sunday. He was not running for any office. not affiliated with any polotical party. wasent looking for votes. had no College degree. wasent bothered about indio China, The Mc-Carthy envestigations or the F.H.A. housing steal. Had his mind on the job at hand and knowed what to do and how to do it. I wondered how the owner could be around something that smart for just A little while and not know A few things himself.

I am talking about A good old honest reliable roping horse. if the man riding him could have done the job as well as the horse they could have roped and tied them calves in nothing flat and had time to spare when behind the barriers kept his eye on that chute gate. and when that dogie left the chute he wasent just ready to go. He was already gone.

It was a pleasure to see something that knowed what to do and done it. wasent scared of being called something he aint.

It would be a wonder now days to see some human that had that much good old hard common sense. know what he wants to do and does it without having to see some bird that wrote some book about something he dident know anything about. but made A lot of research on the matter but that is expecting too much in these days of over education of the wise people. and from A practical point dont know if the Good Lord was crucified or jumped from A aeroplane. And yet we call this the age of enlightment. I dont know. and I am pretty smart. (I think) .

JUNE 3RD, 1954 . . .

Napoleon Bonapart

Ike old boy did cut McCarthy's water off for A few days but his sewer is working again. have at it boys. dont mind the break that is liable to happen between the U. S. and England. Make Mr. Malenkove happy by envestigating how A private in the army got his boots shined. and getting your mug on T.V. we are liable to wake up in the middle of A good fight and wont know what to do. just what Malenkove wants. Divide and conquer. and the allies is divided. or hit before they can consolidate.

Napoleon Bonapart worked that trick and nearly had them all whipped. till he went into Russia and russia whipped him running from him. they put him in shape so the Duke of Wellington could kick the britches off of him at Waterloo. He had covered too much country. we are doing the same thing. Russia is kicking us in the pants so fast the diplomats thinks she is patting for us to dance. we have give them foreign countries groceries, guns and battleships. and if there was A popularity contest between nations now we would be at the bottom. we have tried to buy friendship and respect. that is two commodities that cant be bought. it can be won. but not by our big shots going over in Four motored planes and strawing money around like A drunken Sailor. they think we are A gang of snobs. we have that very bad disease gimmieitis. and it aint getting us any place. one happy consolation, we still have groceries.

JUNE 10TH, 1954 . . .

Degrees

one cinch bet is that I don't know nothing about A literal education. but I can look around me and see that another cinch bet is that when we had to go outside to the toilet: get up at five o'clock in the morning; eat breakfast-not nibble on

Some burnt wind pudding called bread--and sip orange juice; go to the corral; saddle A horse and ride the range; work till sundown; eat supper (and that was before it was called dinner); hit the hot roll and sleep till five o'clock--and do it all over--we was happy.

we had confidence in our fellow man. dident have social security, old age pension and welfare. The country was run by cowmen, lumber men and miners that had brains not degrees. we dident owe anybody anything. we dident have sub Committees and men in THE big capitol telling us how to raise cattle that don't know which end of A cow grazes; that got his knowledge from some book that some bird had wrote that done research on the matter; consulted his attorney and went to see his Dr before putting out the desired information in his bulletin.

and there was no conflict of opinion on their part that it would hurt the welfare of the nation. the biggest thing we had to blow us to hell was a thirty thirty rifle. now we have the atomic bomb that is blowed up higher than A flag on the fourth of July. and we are all just plain scared. dont know what to do or how to do it so it will be legal. and they call this the age of intelligence. I don't know.

JUNE 17TH, 1954 . . .

I Make a Contest and See the Real Thing

I was at A rodeo in the southwestern part of the state last Saturday. Plenty of real Estate was moving, but it was so high in the air that no one was getting any commissions.

the rodeo was by and for range-working cowboys. for that is cow country. and it was easy to see they was the real thing by the suntanned faces and the squinted eyes of them old boys and that they had faced the summer suns and winter snows on the range. their boots shoed signs of having been shined by cow manure. and the chaps of having days of riding in the brush. no loud shirts or fancy stuff at this rodeo.

and there was absent the smell of talcum powder that is so common at the big commercial rodeos of today that is R.C.A. approved. the hearty handshakes was the real McCoy, and the talk was cow talk, like this: "how is your range holding up?" and "do you think the price of cattle will go up?" and once in a while the name of Ezra Benson would come out.

I will have to say I was lost completely. I have been away from that part of life for so long. But I still know A cowboy when I see one. and I seen plenty at that Rodeo. for three days I did not see A T.V. aerial, but plenty of fat white-faced cattle in A world of their own where there was peace and contentment as long as we smart human insects let them alone. it was good to see the real thing again, where there is no sham and shallow pretense. just good old hardworking cowboys.

JUNE 24TH, 1954 . . .

Malenkove Is Happy

well it looks like the mcCarthy bull session is going under cover but the effects of that Squabble (over nothing that I can see) will remain for A long time. if that old joker had of put as much effort in CONSTRUCTING confidence in the American people, as well as our Allies, as he has DESTRUCTING confidence, he might have worked wonders. but he seems to be the bull of the woods and there is nothing we can do about it I reckon.

And lets hope and pray (tho it will be in vain) that we dont have another round like the McCarthy deal. there is another boiling now--the Oppenheimer thing. aint that silly. I would lay A bet that he knows more about the Atomic bomb than any man in the U.S.

it just appears to me (tho I am not Smart) that A bunch of the high Diplomats in Washington D. C. is A bunch of over-educated half wits, looking for votes and publicity. and France changing premiers so fast that one don't get hungry till there is A new one elected. well that is something they do to save the feed bill on them. is shore making Malenkove happy. that is something.

<small>JULY 1ST</small>, 1954 . . .

Eleven Shot Six Shooters

I went to see one of these blood and thunder western movies the other day. and I just had to laugh out loud. if you cant pull A pistol from off each hip and fan both of them at the same time and hit the bulls eye every time you are A sissy. if you cant kiss the woman and make it sound like a cow pulling her foot out of A bog you are not A cowboy, and if you cant knock the liver out of at least five men without getting your hair messed up you are out of date.

The hero was A football half back, quarter back or broke back. and I would lay A bet that he has never been out of A town only on location, and then had someone to keep him from getting lost. he rode A horse that didnt know how to walk. he run for hours at A time. that horse shore was long winded, and when the big stampede come off there was one old holstein steer that I know come before that Camera four times.

they had an awful time getting them old gentle steers to run at all. the hero had been in camp for months and was still smoking Taylor made Cigarettes and wearing a wrist watch. the Time was 75 years ago. I guess helicopters was dropping cigarettes and keeping him informed about the right time so he could set his watch. I suppose he was A union man and just worked eight hours A day. and had to have his watch to see that he dident work overtime. the picture show was packed so I guess it is all right. and I got my moneys worth in good laughs, so what.

JULY 15TH, 1954 . . .

Over the 4th of July, while the great, and them that is wanting to be great, was blowing off about patriotism and what ort to be done--which was ninety percent bull and ten percent promises--I was looking at something that had some sense . . . a string of good fat steers on a real ranch in Colorado. Full of good grass and water, with nothing to do but switch their tails to shoo the flies away. I was looking at them from the air foam seat of a lincoln automobile. I can just imagine what them old fat steers was saying to themselves: you silly fools, I am contented, full of grass and water and not trying to best someone out of something. When I get hungry I eat. I don't want to go no place. You entelligent birds have big automobiles that can play making seventy five miles per hour. get your vitamins shot into your arms. Always in A hurry trying to beat somebody out of something or going to see your attorney. dont know where you are going half the time and dont know the other half of the time when you get there.

and I wonder if them old fat steers aint right. for the big ranch house had eight bedrooms in it. there was the up-stairs. downstairs and basement. too big to live in and not big enough for A hotel. I bogged to my knees in the rugs on the floors. Oh yes, it had a bar, too.

My opinion (not worth much) is that them steers has got more good common hard sense than the man that owns the ranch. he is trying to get his lunch grabbers on all the money in the world. the steers is content with A good living. I wonder if this is the age of intelligence.

AUGUST 5TH, 1954 . . .

See Bricker Not Webster

A lawyer friend of mine gave me A book. name of it is The Bricker amendment. I have labored over that fool thing for

A week; Wrecked my poor inefficient brain trying to figure out the Whereases, Concurrent Resolutions, Coddicils and Precedents that is laid out in that little thing. And I have decided two things: it was made for lawyers by lawyers and of lawyers. So the great American language can be all messed up with that pig latin lingo so that the common dung hill wont savvy what it is all about. the second thing I decided is that the Taxpayer is the corpus delecti, and after the men of the Great legal profession gets done arguing over it, and has spent all the money they meant to on it, They will do with it just as they want to.

One thing I shore dont savvy is that them men of the legal profession go to school most of their life and dont learn the American language but have to fall back on some latin stuff that would have been gone and forgotten long ago if it wasnt for the fact that they have to talk that lingo to keep the man that is paying the bill from knowing what they are saying. I wonder why they dont get one of doughBelly's Scrapbooks and learn the english language as it is spoken by the general run of people today; come down out of that great cloud of legal hokus pocus and be somebody.

but I reckon that is too much to expect of them. they have been to school so much and nobody would know it if they talked like other people. I shore wish I was one of them, as that is the best graft I know of anywhere. but if it had not been for lawyers I would be making little rocks out of big ones today; not because I was not guilty but because I had A good mouthpiece. more power to the men of the legal Prof.

AUGUST 7TH, 1954 . . .

What a Life

I shore did punish my old Belly Sat. I went to one of them democratic Barbeques. The beef we eat was following A cow A month ago but he was not looking for milk. I have seen bulls crippled worse than that was and get well.

I shook hands with plenty of them Candidates that had A big smile on their face that should have had A big Number on their back. And all of them is looking for A chance to muddle up our business for A term. what A grand time the F.B.I. could have had envestigating that gang of rounders, roughnecks, hack drivers, politicians, lawyers and Drs. I had to use Colorax to get the stink off my hands after shaking all them polluted lunch grabbers that was shoved at me that day. Big picket was dealing out his cards, and dealing from the top, I think, and I should know.

I left before the speeches. No smarter than I am I knowed what the speeches would consist of. NOW LADIES AND GENTLEMEN OF THE DEMOCRATIC PARTY (they would have to enclude that democratic party so the people would know what they was) we are here to fight our common enemy, the republicans. APPLAUSE. and the speaker would grin like A cat eating liver. we must give the country back to the democratic party. (more applause and A bigger grin) AND RETURN PROSPERITY TO THE PEOPLE of the great State of New Mexico and the nation. (the speaker licks his lips and buttons his coat), looks the crowd over like A mule at A motherless colt and proceeds with more of the S.O.S. (same old stuff) that we have had put to us for years. I fully agree with that Radio program . . . people are funny, and A little dumb.

there was one republican there. he should be awarded the purple heart for bravery beyond the call of duty. his hip pocket was bulging but I think it was A pint of whiskey not A pistol. and his feed cost him A buck. it might have been tainted but the Demos took it just the same. they just dont turn them Dollars no way but down into the campaign funds.

Cads and Protruding Bellies

I shore am glad to see the approaching death of the eighty-third Congress. It has suffered so long and had such Terrible pains. Spent millions of dollars for TV time trying to find out who shined the Army private's shoes, who got the money and what went with it; days and days of argument over farm parity--whatever that is. It is high time it was laid to rest.

The Democrats is doing a lot of Heehawing about A depression--that dont look just right to me. This is the first time in years that there was not A shooting war going on somewhere. the US is bringing three divisions home from Korea. you have got to get on the waiting list for months to buy A cadillac automobile. nearly everyone you meet is trying to reduce in weight-their bellies sticking out like A poisoned pup's from overeating.

But the demos say the dirty republicans is ruining the country. if this is ruination of the country, I shore would like to see it keep going to ruin.

Long may Ike Eisenhower live. may his golf game improve, and above all let us pray that he has better tools to work with in the next session of congress.

P. S. I am A democrat, nearly.

CHAPTER FIVE

SHOW TIME *by doughBelly Price*

The Spring after I was fourteen years old, I had come to the conclusion that I was the best bronc rider in the world. Though no one else thought so didn't make any difference to me.

I got me a job riding broncs and cooking on a little Mud Show. It was called Wild West, more wild than West, and the term Mud Show means that we went over land and eat some of the time. The balance of the time we either went hungry or stole what we had to eat.

It was a little carnival we was with and on that aggregation of rounders, roughnecks and thieves was one of them hula hula shows as was the case in most all of the shows them days.

The Wild West Show was getting enough money most of the time so we could eat, mostly liver and onions; but that was good when you was hungry, till both of the bosses fell for the hula hula girl. She was one of them kind with the hue colored hair, a bad case of the T. B. (terrific butt) and could she shake it, as she had plenty to shake. Her idea was that when she stepped out on the bally platform, the world should bow low and paw dirt over their shoulders and bellow. After that just as soon as a show was pulled and a little money come our way, the first one to the ticket box would take the bank roll and away to the tent of the hula hula girl. Of course, the one that got to the ticket seller last was out in the cold and was not liable to be any bother that night.

The bucking horses started to getting thin and the cowboys thinner. There is a code of all cowboys -- "Feed the horse" -- and all of the bronc riders in that show was or had been cowboys on the range. Tho' in later years some of the so-called cowboys in shows didn't know if a cow roosted in trees or slept on the ground.

Things finally come to a showdown on the 4th of July night. We had had a good day and there was a little money for both men so they met near the tent of the hula girl, both armed to the gills and ready for battle and both carrying pistols that was used around the show to shoot soap wads in for a racket when we was ballyhooing. The barrel of both guns was pretty badly soaped up and I guess that is the reason there was nine shots and not a score made, therefore no blood.

The two bosses' names was Tetters and Naves. Naves was in the tent ahead of Tetters that night and heard Tetters telling another carnival thug what he was going to do to Naves for playing with his girl. Naves slipped into his boots and pants and buckled on the trusty forty-four and come forth to battle for the honor of the girl he loved.

By that time Tetters had got the load off his chset to the carnival thug and started towards the tent where he was confident that he would find the villian that he was seeking. When he was about twenty yards from the portable home of his desired one, out steps Naves and said,

"Pard, are you armed?"

And he opened fire. Me and another one of the bronc riders was unrolling our beds in the cook's tent that also served as a bedroom, not forty feet from either one, but out of line of fire when it started and I thought the Civil War had broke out again. Each shot was slow and seemed like each man was taking his time. And to hear them old (both guns was forty-fours) forty some odd slugs whine and cry as they winged their way to nowhere was not a pleasant thing; so me and the other boy took to cover by rolling up in our beds. Finally the smoke cleared away. Both guns was empty and we had got up courage enough to stick our heads out under the sidewall of the tent and they was flailing each other over the heads with the empty guns.

The hula girl was throwing a fit and the whole carnival was out to see what was going on. The fight was stopped and neither had done the other any damage to speak of, but here come the limb of the law and both went to jail.

The carnival moved on a day or two, but not the Wild West Show, as both bosses was in the clink and there was no guiding hand to steer the mighty show on its way.

The hula girl was held for some kind of witness and me and the other boy that had heard all of it and seen a little was also held as witnesses the same as the girl; but not locked up, as the jail only had two cells and Naves and Tetters had to be kept separate. They was kept in the cells and the girl had the rest of the clink to herself. She kept busy going from one cell to the other telling first one and then the other how much she loved him and how she would stay with him till death do us part if she had to conk him on the noggin herself, and then to the other cell and tell the other one about the same thing and then set back and listen at them rave at one another.

After four days, the morning of the trial come around. We all met in the little Justice's office and the comedy started. Both men had hired a mouthpiece and give him all the money they had, so it made very little difference what was done with the men.

The trial lasted all day and just as the evening sun made its last dip for the day, the summations was concluded and the verdict was give.

Tetters had somehow stashed away a ten dollar bill and that was brought to light during the trial and he was fined that ten.

Naves was broke so he was turned loose and the court

made each one of the men promise not to do no more shooting in the city limits.

The girl was fined eight dollars and seventy cents. It was found out that she had that much for disorderly conduct, provided she get out of town.

The city marshal went to the show ground to see that there was no shooting while the Wild West Show was divided. That was not hard.

Naves owned a big monkey, one paint stud and one old gentle mare and a bucking horse called Cyclone Dick; also a light wagon and a very few pots and pans.

The girls stayed with Tetters, so none of us wanted to go along so we throwed in our lot with Naves and the big monkey. I have often thought that the monkey was just as bad as the girl, but not knowing just how bad she was, I am in no position to say if we made a bad deal or not.

Some of the boys purloined enough of the show canvas to make a top over the wagon and we put the big monkey in the cage in the very backend, tied Dick behind the wagon and started back to Wichita Falls, Texas, some one hundred and fifty miles to get the ingredients for another show.

Another rider landed on the show the day after the shooting and he went along back to help start the new show. When we got to a town where there was as many as ten people we would ride the bucking horse for a hat collection no matter what the collection amounted to and stole most of the feed from farmers to feed the stock.

One afternoon we boys was playing cards in the space between the spring seat and the monkey cage (and that monkey would nibble on you. No one could do anything with him but Naves). We got thirsty and played a game of pitch to see who would get out at the next farm house and get a bucket of water. The new rider lost and at the next house he got out and got a bucket of water from the lady of the house.

Naves was driving as he thought no one but him had sense enough to drive that stud. When we all got a drink there was some water left in the bucket. The little stud was standing with his head down about all in. The new man leveled off with what was left of the water, hit that stud just below where the tail comes off, and he woke up with a jar. Around he went and turned the wagon over her, me, the big boy that was in the tent when the shooting was going on and a trick roper hemmed in between the spring seat and the monkey cage. The cage door come open and here we are; the monkey, the roper, and me, every fellow playing his own part and the monkey with the high hand for I only weighed about one hundred pounds so I didn't have much trouble making a hole out through the top of that canvas on the wagon and had two followers immediately.

By the time we got the stud settled down he was all in for sure. Naves asked the woman if we could camp and get water at the well.

She said, "No," and in a way that there was no room for argument. I can't say that I blamed her in the least.

Naves got the monk in his cell and there was only one thing to do, that was hitch the great bucking horse to the wagon and see what happened. Plenty did! The old big boy, my pard in crime, eared him down and I throwed the harness on him. That was when things got rushing. Big boy could hold the front end down, but that back end was shore working high in the air. I stepped back to give that back end room to work and heard a peculiar sound from the porch of the house where we got the water and looked to see what was happening there. The woman was down on her knees and I never seen no one laughing as hard as she was. Her husband had come running from the field to see what was going on and seen part of it.

When the dust cleared, the woman said, "Yes, you can camp inside the pasture and I will get you boys a good supper as a show like that is worth a week's board for all of you.

We had a grand supper, the horses a real feed, and we did not hit the bedroll till twelve o'clock that night. We just set on the porch and talked.

The next morning the stud was able to hold up his side of the wagon tongue, the old mare could pull the load, and we was on our way.

The trick roper had a new Stetson hat that he was very proud of and he had tied it up to the wagon bows in the top of the wagon and had appropriated him a little derby that just set up on the cheap side of his head.

We was camped on a little stream of water two miles from a little town and we had took up a hat collection that afternoon and had money to buy liver and onions. The roper mounted the stud and went to town after the groceries and old Naves had tied the monkey to a bush with a thirty foot light chain. He seen the roper coming back with the sack of grub. He went to work pulling the chain in and laying it down. I was watching him and wondering what he was up to. When the roper got close enough, the monkey made a jump and went right up behind the saddle on the Stud's rump, and the fireworks started. The stud bucked the roper off right straight on his head and jammed that derby so far down, it took two of us to pull him from under it.

The sack of grub was the first thing the roper discarded and by the time we got the stud under control and the derby pulled off the roper. The monkey had gone all the way through the sack of stuff. The roper was the maddest man I think I ever saw. He said either he or the monkey had to go. The monkey stayed.

This is just one of the many many happenings that I have seen in the show business. It gets in the blood. I sometimes now get to thinking back over them days and laugh like the fool that I am. I would not take plenty for what I have learned with shows; but would not go back over them times for plenty.

www.ingramcontent.com/pod-product-compliance
Lightning Source LLC
Chambersburg PA
CBHW020403130626
46549CB00006B/2425